GOD'S PROGRAM
OF THE AGES

God's Program
of the Ages

by

Frederick A. Tatford, Litt.D.

KREGEL PUBLICATIONS
GRAND RAPIDS, MICHIGAN 49501

Library of Congress Catalog Card Number 67-26075

ISBN 0-8254-3801-2

First Edition 1967
Second Printing 1968
Third Printing 1971

Printed in the United States of America

Foreword

When Professor Stewart was asked recently what, in his opinion, would be the principal emphasis in preaching during the next decade, he replied unhesitatingly that it would be eschatology. With this estimate many theologians would agree, whatever their personal interpretation of the *eschaton*. Since the World Council of Churches assembly at Evanston in 1955, Protestant theology has devoted increasing attention to this subject, even though it has been stated that only ten per cent find any vital significance in the doctrine of the Second Advent. Yet, as Dr. Carl F. H. Henry says, "Hope in the future lends such a meaning to life that even where the Christian revelation is unknown, men and women dream of some new era of promise. Western scientism and Marxist communism have stripped all supernatural features from the vision of a coming kingdom, have linked it exclusively to the forces of nature and history, and have promised modern man an earthly paradise of material prosperity and security. Thus confidence, either in forces supposedly immanent in nature and history or in man's ability to exploit such forces, has become the foundation of this era's hope for meaningful survival and destiny." There is all the more reason, therefore, to recover and proclaim the Biblical revelation concerning the last things.

This has become all the more essential because of the uncertainty regarding the world's future which is troubling the minds of men today. The possibility — which can never be completely ignored — of nuclear warfare, the dread of new thermonuclear devices, the constant friction between the peoples of the world, and the stress and tensions of international relations, all provide an incentive to look beyond the present into the future. The utopian expectations and hopes, to which the end of the last war gave rise, seem to have been strangled at birth. If this life is the end, the outlook is gloomy indeed. There must be something beyond. The inspiration for the present lies not in the glory of the past but in the hope of the future.

The hope of many a simple Christian is in the return of his Lord and Saviour, and this is not really surprising. As Dr. Clovis G. Chappell says, "Since the early saints believed in the immediate and visible return of Jesus, it is not a matter of wonder that many earnest and devout men and women have held to this faith throughout the centuries. There are those who believe it joyfully today." Here indeed is the only reply to the soul's deepest longing, the only answer to the cares and worries of earthly life, the only solution to problems too great for man to solve. Christ is the final answer to human need.

It was nine years since Agamemnon had set out to attack and destroy the city of Troy, and back at Argos the sentry paced the flat roof of the palace, constantly awaiting the firing of a distant beacon as an indication of the king's return. There seemed no end to the long, weary vigil. Would the king never return? But one night a tongue of flame shot up from the crest of the distant hill — the long-expected sign of the coming of the king. Fatigue banished, the long days and nights of waiting forgotten, the soldier shouted in ecstatic joy, "Rejoice, rejoice! Hail, thou auspicious flame, that streaming through the night proclaimest joy." The victory had been won, and the king had returned. The palace was filled with joy. We also wait. Our Master's coming seems to have been so long delayed; sometimes our hearts grow weary and our hopes grow faint and perhaps even doubt begins to descend upon us. Will He never come? Is His return to be postponed until the fulfilment of predicted events, or is His coming imminent?

There can be no question as to the certainty of the Second Advent, but many are not clear regarding its place in the Divine program and consequently whether it may be expected in the near future or must necessarily be long delayed. It is hoped that the following chapters will clarify the sequence of events in the Divine plan and help to confirm the sure basis of the Christian hope.

FREDERICK A. TATFORD

Contents

CHAPTER I. # The Interpretation of Prophecy

THERE IS a natural instinct which impels men to probe into the future and to seek to discover its hidden mysteries, and the dreads and uncertainties of our twentieth century have given purpose to the search. It is not surprising that the Christian, faced with similar problems and difficulties, should turn to the Bible to ascertain what God has revealed through His Word. Consequently, the prophetic writings today occupy a place of far greater importance in the eyes of the church than ever in past history, due primarily, of course, to their relevance to the present day.

Nevertheless, there is a danger that, in occupation with the details and symbols of the prophetic Word, the underlying principles of God's dealings may be overlooked. H. H. Rowley has pertinently remarked in *The Relevance of Apocalyptic* that those who refuse to study the canonical apocalyptic books, "as wholes can never discern the profound and enduring spiritual principles on which they are based, while the obsession with the equation of the words of Scripture with the events of our day converts the books into intricate puzzles for the ingenious, instead of spiritual messages to harassed souls. . . . They are Divine messages, addressed indeed to the age in which they were composed, but addressed also to every age. The visions of Daniel and of the Book of Revelation merit attention, not alone to the details of their form, but to the great spiritual principles which they everywhere assume." If we lose sight of the principles in an obsession with the details, we defraud ourselves of the essential value of this inspired literature. It is more important for the Word of God to have its effect upon our lives and conduct than for us to be able to give an accurate outline of the Divine program for the future. The ways of God with the man Nebuchadnezzar, for example, are probably of more vital import than the Divine revelation to the Chaldean king of the course of world empires. The unveiling in the Apocalypse of the glory and pre-eminence of Christ is more pertinent to the spiritual man than an understanding of the place in prophecy of the two Beasts of Revelation 13.

It is, nevertheless, a fact that a considerable portion of the Scriptures is concerned with "the last things" and that its prophetic significance cannot be ignored. Moreover, from a practical point of view, the Biblical prophecies provide the greatest incentive to Christian life and service and the greatest inspiration to hope and sanctification. During the early days of Christianity, the Advent hope as Froom remarks was, "the sustaining strength of the martyr church. It was profound belief in her Lord's return, assured by His own promise and by the outline prophecies, that nerved her to face the fierce persecutions of a hostile pagan state."

During the first three centuries of the Christian era, the belief was general that there would soon be a literal and personal return of our Lord and that this Second Advent would be to destroy the Antichrist and his followers and to introduce the millennium. In his *History of the Christian Church*, Philip Schaff says, "The most striking point in the eschatology of the ante-Nicene age is the prominent Chiliasm or millenarianism, that is, the belief in a visible reign of Christ in glory on earth with the risen saints for a thousand years, before the general resurrection and judgment." The Lord's return was expected imminently. Before the end of the first century, Clement of Rome was expressing a belief in the early return of the Master, and in 100 A.D., the Didache was stressing the need for watchfulness in the light of that event. It is true that the Epistle of Barnabas and the Shepherd of Hermas both envisaged the Church passing through the great tribulation before the Lord's return, and that Irenaeus, who was a disciple of Polycarp (a contemporary of the apostle John), taught that Antichrist's reign and the great tribulation would be followed by the coming of Christ to establish His kingdom; but whatever the church's views on the great tribulation, the return and consequent reign of Christ were the constant hope of the Christian. The primitive church accepted Chiliasm almost universally, and it is interesting to note that the opponents of this view were mainly the early heretics, e.g., the gnostics, Platonists and Montanists.

The original chiliastic belief was first attacked by Origen (185-254 A.D.), who introduced a spiritual or allegorical method of interpretation. He considered that the triumph of Christianity over the world was not to be effected by a Divine interposition but, on the contrary, by a long and gradual process, and he refused to interpret literally the Scriptural references to the millennium. His spiritualizing method is evidenced in his statement in his *Commentaries on Matthew*, "there comes daily, to the soul of every believer, the second advent of the Word in the prophetic clouds, that is, in the writings of the prophets and apostles, which reveal Him and in all their words disclose the light of truth, and declare Him as coming forth in their significations." The concerted efforts of Origen and later of his disciple, Dionysius of Alexandria, to destroy the early belief of the Church served to arouse many, and chiliasm remained the belief of a large number, and we find writers like Tertullian (150-225 A.D.) maintaining that, after the resurrection of believers, there will be a literal thousand year theocratic kingdom upon earth.

When Constantine (272-337 A.D.) became emperor of the Roman Empire and also embraced the Christian faith, the persecution which the church had suffered was suddenly replaced by imperial patronage and material prosperity. The advent hope waned, and many were persuaded that their expectations had been realized and that they had already entered the earthly millennium. The change of attitude is exemplified in Eusebius Pamphili (260-340 A.D.), the Bishop of Caesarea and the father of church history. In his *Proof of the Gospel,* Eusebius taught that there would be a literal Second Advent of Christ to establish the kingdom of God on earth. After Constantine's conversion, Eusebius took the view in his later books, *Life of Constantine* and *Ecclesiastical History,* that the kingdom had already come. There were a few, however, like Lactantius (240-330 A.D.) who expressed the view in his *Divine Institutions* about 310 A.D., that the church would suffer the troubles of the end-time but that 6,000 years of history would be followed by 1,000 years of Christ's reign.

The teaching of Origen's followers received a very great impetus from Aurelius Augustine (354-430), Bishop of Hippo. Augustine adopted the theory of Tichonius, whose commentary on the Apocalypse in the latter part of the fourth century suggested that the millennium dated from the first advent of Christ. In *The City of God* Augustine took the line that the kingdom of God referred to the church ruling on earth. The first resurrection he regarded as spiritual and not literal, and Babylon was to be identified with Rome. The millennium ran from Christ's first advent up to His second coming, and Satan was bound for the whole of that period. Considerable spiritualizing of many of the prophecies was entailed in order to make them fit in with the scheme of interpretation. Although the millennial belief of the early church continued through the centuries, it was very largely superseded by the allegorical teaching of Origen and Augustine, and Christians in general were satisfied to find the fulfilment of prophecy in the triumph of the Church.

The character of the Popes and the veniality of the papal curia, however, gave rise to no little doubt and disquiet, and at the end of the tenth century, we find Arnulf, Bishop of Orleans, and others equally outspoken, referring to the Pope as Antichrist. In the twelfth century Bernard of Cluny described the Pope as "king of this odious Babylon", and similar expressions were used by Robert Grossteste, Bishop of Lincoln, Pierre Jean d'Olivi and a host of others.

It was difficult for the more spiritual leaders to accept the idea that the domination of the church of Rome was identical with the millennial kingdom of prophecy, and they began to call into question the Augustinian allegorization. Joachim of Floris (1130-1202), who gave himself to the study of prophecy, finally rejected Augustine's interpretation and declared that a new age was to be expected in which life would be elevated to a higher spiritual plane. He referred to Rome as Babylon and to the Pope as Antichrist. According to L. Berkhof (*The Second Coming of Christ*), he taught that, "the age of the Spirit was destined to begin in the year 1260 A.D. Then the church would be purified; Jews and Gentiles would be converted in great masses; and a final conflict would be waged against the evil forces of the world, and then the new order would begin under the blessed reign of Jesus Christ." The thirteenth century Joachimite school consistently referred to the Pope as Antichrist and to the Roman Catholic system as Babylon. Fourteenth century stalwarts like John Wycliffe and John Huss used similar expressions, and these were repeated in the succeeding two centuries by Martin Luther, William Tyndale, John Calvin and many another.

The corruption of Rome in the Middle Ages led to a rising flood of denunciation, and it was increasingly maintained that many of the apocalyptic symbols were appropriate to her. To a great extent, it was the revived study of the Biblical prophecies and the conviction that so much of them was applicable to Papal Rome that led to the Reformation of 1500 to 1650. Prophetic interpretation during the Middle Ages was largely along historicist lines, and this continued through the Reformation period, until the propounding of very different bases of interpretation by the Roman Catholic Church. Even when Martin Luther had first made his anti-papal protest, the Catholic doctors Prierias and Eck had, to quote Froom, "boldly reasserted the Lateran theory and declared the papal dominion to be Daniel's fifth monarchy, or reign of the saints, and identified the existing Roman church with the New Jerusalem." But the Reformers had been universally unanimous in their condemnation of Rome and the Papacy as Babylon and Antichrist, and their statements were reiterated in the books and tracts which were being poured out. So clear did the identification seem that the cumulative effect could have been catastrophic for Rome, but for her Jesuit Counter — Reformation of the sixteenth and seventeenth centuries.

The historicist interpretation had been the basis of the Protestant attack upon Rome. The latter's only defence must be on prophetic grounds; by some means or other it must be demonstrated that Antichrist and Babylon had no relevance to the present. "The symbols must be pushed out of the entire field of medieval contemporary history." But how? Two conflicting theories were propounded, each calculated to destroy confidence — albeit in totally different ways — in the historicist view. The first is commonly referred to as the futurist interpretation, and the other as the preterist.

In 1590, Francisco Ribera (1537-1591), a Jesuit of Salamanca, issued a commentary on the Apocalypse (of which a synopsis is given in E. B. Elliott's *Horae Apocalypticae*) in which he reverted to the futurist view of the early Fathers. He maintained that the Antichrist would arise not long before Christ's return and could not, therefore, have any reference to existing individuals or systems. Arguing from Revelation 17:16, that the papacy would be destroyed before the coming of Antichrist, he referred the Babylon of Revelation 18 to a future pagan and apostate Rome. Ribera's teaching was carried further by Cardinal Robert Bellarmine (1542-1621), who showed that the early Christians believed in a literal three and one-half years' rule by Antichrist and not in the 1260 years (on the year-day basis) proposed by the Protestants. Bellarmine also argued that Antichrist must be a Jew, located at Jerusalem and not at Rome.

A very different line was taken by Luis de Alcazar (1554-1613), a Jesuit of Seville. If Ribera thrust Antichrist and Babylon into the future, Alcazar thrust them back into the past. In a commentary on the Apocalypse, published posthumously in 1614, he took the view that the Revelation was concerned with the conflict of the early church with the Jews on the one hand and with pagan Rome on the other, Antichrist being identified with Nero. It was quite clear that, if his view was accepted, there could be no reference in prophecy to Papal Rome. Alcazar's preterist view was adopted by Hugo Grotius (1583-1645), a Protestant of Holland, in a book published in 1644, and it was subsequently adopted by rationalist scholars such as G. H. A. Ewald (1803-1875), W. L. M. de Wette (1780-1849), F. Delitzsch (1813-1890), and J. Wellhausen (1844-1918).

Three schools of prophetic interpretation were thus in existence in the Post-Reformation period. These three — the preterist, the historicist and the futurist — are usually referred to, for obvious reasons, as chronological schools of interpretation.

The preterist view is no longer widely held, but the historicist still prevails in many quarters. In his *Key of the Revelation,* J. Mede (1586-1638) reverted to the historicist year-day basis, but he declared that the millennium was still future, thus repudiating the Augustinian teaching that the thousand years (including the binding of Satan) commenced with Christ's first advent. Bishop T. Newton (1704-

1782) followed a similar line in his *Dissertations on the Prophecies*. In 1740 J. A. Bengel (1687-1752) issued a commentary on the Revelation which showed that, although he was a premillennialist, he also belonged to the historicist school. His exposition was closely followed by John Wesley (1703-1791). The majority of the historicist school believe in the return of our Lord to establish a literal kingdom on earth. Eschatologically, therefore, they belong to the premillennial school.

Ribera's futurist interpretation was espoused in the nineteenth century by S. R. Maitland (1792-1866) in a pamphlet issued in 1826, "An Enquiry into the ground on which the prophetic period of Daniel and St. John has been supposed to consist of 1260 years," which attacked the year-day basis. The Oxford Tractarian Movement (1833-1845), a High Church body, also adopted the futurist view, particularly as regards the Antichrist, and used it as an argument for reunion with Rome. The futurist basis of interpretation is still widely held and has become closely associated with the premillennial school.

Just as there are three chronological schools of interpretation, so there are three eschatological schools — the post-millennial, the a-millennial and the pre-millennial.

Postmillennialism may be traced back to certain teachings of Augustine in the fourth century, but its development is due primarily to Daniel Whitby (1638-1726). Whitby was the originator of modern postmillennialism in his *Paraphrase and Commentary on the New Testament* published in 1703. In this he taught that, through the outpouring of the Holy Spirit, the world would gradually be converted and that then the thousand years of the millennium would be enjoyed before the return of our Lord. C. Vitringa (1659-1722), Count N. L. Zindendorf and many others became adherents of this school. Since this teaching made the golden age dependent, not upon a Divine intervention, but upon the conversion of the world through human effort, it is not surprising that social reformation began to take the place of the gospel. "The emphasis on social reform increased at the expense of Christian doctrine," says Froom, "and the postmillennial hopes of progressive righteousness became allied with the humanistic and evolutionary doctrine of human progress. Thus postmillennialism tended to line up with modernism, with the credal element virtually disappearing, and the main emphasis on church union and the social gospel." The spiritual vacuity of the message became apparent in the first World War, which completely destroyed any notion that the world was getting better and better, and postmillennialism as such is not extremely popular today.

To some extent, amillennialism has grown out of postmillennialism. Certainly, like the latter, it found its roots in Augustine's theories. Unlike postmillennialism, it does not expect the world to be converted before the Second Advent. The amillennial school teaches that the kingdom of God is heavenly and not earthly and that the thousand years of Revelation 20 are not intended to be a literal millennium of earthly blessing. The kingdom, it is alleged, was inaugurated at the first advent of Christ, and its subjects are members of the church and not of the nation of Israel as such, since there is no future for the nation. There will be a general resurrection of the dead at the return of Christ to the earth when all will be judged and a new heaven and a new earth brought into being. Allis, for example, says, "that the only visible coming of Christ to this earth which the church is to expect will be for judgment, and will be followed by the final state." The adherents of this school are increasing in number and include such leaders as O. T. Allis, L. Berkhof, B. B. Warfield, and well-known men in England.

The amillennial view has left many minds unsatisfied, however, and one result has been the development of what has been termed "realized eschatology". In *The Parables of the Kingdom,* for example, C. H. Dodd suggests that our Lord's parables and sayings make it clear that the kingdom of God has already come. It "has moved from the future to the present, from the sphere of expectation into that of realized experience." "The predictions of Jesus have no long historical perspective," he says. "They seem to be concerned with the immediate developments of the crisis which was already in being when He spoke, and which He interpreted as the coming of the kingdom of God." In *The Mystery of the Kingdom of God,* A. Schweitzer declared, "The death of Jesus is the end of eschatology," and that Jesus expected a miraculous intervention of God in His own lifetime to terminate human history and to inaugurate the kingdom. In *Jesus and His Coming,* J. A. T. Robinson says that our Lord's "concern was with the present moment, with the crisis introduced into history by the advent of the kingdom of God, at work proleptically in His ministry and shortly to be fulfilled in His death." That the Bishop of Woolwich does not believe in the Second Advent is clear when he writes, "Jesus, vindicated by God as Lord and Christ from the moment of the resurrection, reigns henceforth till all His foes submit, and in the Spirit He has poured forth the power by which this is to be accomplished. This reign has yet indeed to reach its consummation in the final day of the Lord and in the judgment to which, already, Jesus has been appointed by God. But there is no hint of a second messianic event in history and no idea of the Christ coming again. . . . There is but one coming, begun at Christmas, perfected on the Cross, and continuing till all are included in it."

Although premillennialism may be traced back to the early days of the church, its revival is due in no small measure to a Spanish Jesuit named Manuel da Lacunza (1731-1801). Lacunza was not satisfied with the common Roman Catholic thesis from the days of Augustine that the millennium began either at our Lord's first advent or at the conversion of Constantine. In consequence of his personal Bible study, he issued *The Coming of Messiah in Glory and Majesty* in manuscript form in 1791 under the pseudonym of J. J. Ben-Ezra. In this he taught that the Second Advent would precede the millennium and that there would be two resurrections separated by 1,000 years. Edward Irving (1792-1834) was greatly affected by the book and translated it into English and tabled it for discussion at the first of the prophetic conferences held from 1826 to 1830 at Henry Drummond's house at Albury Park, near Guildford. The book also played a part in the formation in 1826 of the Society for the Investigation of Prophecy, which later became the Prophecy Investigation Society, continuing under this name until 1964. Lady Powerscourt, who attended the Albury Park conferences, started similar meetings at Powerscourt Castle in 1830.

In the three volumes of *Dialogues on Prophecy*, issued after the Albury Park meetings, there were references implying a "rapture" of the church before the great tribulation, and this was certainly discussed at the Powerscourt meetings. In *The Hope of Christ's Second Coming*, S. P. Tregelles alleged that the idea of the rapture was introduced by Irving and that he derived it from utterances in "tongues", but this was never definitely substantiated. It is also alleged that Joseph Mede held the rapture theory two centuries earlier, having derived it from a Jewish tradition, but this is also unsupported.

The premillennialist's conception of the order of future events has been concisely summarized by W. J. Grier in *The Momentous Event*, although not all premillennialists would agree in every detail. His summary is as follows: "(1) A period of apostasy preceding the Lord's coming. (2) The Lord will come in secret, and will raise the dead saints, snatching them away together with the living believers — an event commonly called the 'secret rapture'. (3) There will ensue a short seven year period of great tribulation, in which the Antichrist will rule the earth. (4) Then Christ will appear from heaven openly, Armageddon will be fought and Christ will overthrow Antichrist and the hosts of evil. This will usher in the Redeemer's glorious reign at Jerusalem, and the temple and the sacrificial worship will be restored. (5) At the end of the thousand years, Satan will be loosed again and will stir up rebellion against God. His crushing defeat will be followed by the resurrection of the wicked and their judgment and the eternal state."

Some elements of truth are to be found in each theory, and they cannot be lightly dismissed because our own inclination is towards a particular one. A study of the progress of dogma shows that in the early centuries of church history attention was focused first on apologetics, then on theology, then anthropology and later on Christology, these being followed by soteriology and ecclesiology, and it was not until the last century that much notice was given to eschatology. In some respects, final views on this subject may not even yet have crystallized.

 # The Dispensations

"DISTINGUISH THE ages," said Augustine, "and the Scriptures harmonize," and in *Major Bible Themes*, L. S. Chafer maintains that the Bible is divisible into certain well-defined periods of time, or dispensations, and that, "the recognition of these divisions with their divine purposes constitutes one of the most important factors in true interpretation of the Scriptures." It must indeed be apparent, even to the most superficial reader, that God's relations with earth and His governmental dealings with man have not continued immutably and without variation since time began, but that changes in divine requirements and alterations in emphasis on human responsibilities have occurred at specific points of time — and with the patent object that different tests might be imposed upon mankind. Every dispensation, as one writer remarks, "begins with man divinely placed in a new position of privilege and responsibility, and closes with the failure of man resulting in righteous judgment from God." These time periods or dispensations, as G. H. Pember rightly remarks in *The Great Prophecies of the Centuries*, "all combine to prove that, in no conceivable circumstances, is man able to preserve or recover his integrity, and to save himself from corruption; that his sole hope lies in a direct interposition of the Eternal, and so wonderful an infusion of the Holy Spirit that an entire change is wrought in his nature."

This principle of interpretation is not a new one. In *A Bibliographic History of Dispensationalism*, Arnold Ehlert traces the history of dispensational schemes of interpretation down the centuries and shows that quite early in church history there was a clear recognition of God's dispensational dealings with earth, although subsequent development led to a more precise definition of these Biblical divisions than at first.

What is commonly termed modern dispensationalism seems to have originated primarily in prophetic conferences which first came into being in the last century. As mentioned in chapter one, from 1826 to 1830 conferences of this kind were held from time to time at Henry Drummond's villa at Albury Park, Guildford. In addition to Drummond himself, Hugh McNeile, Joseph Wolff, Lord Mandeville and other keen ministers and evangelists attended the meetings. Similar conferences were commenced in Ireland at Powerscourt Castle by Lady Powerscourt and continued from 1830 to 1838. Here Biblical students and teachers, such as Dr. S. P. Tregelles, Sir Edward Denny, J. N. Darby, Edward Irving and B. W. Newton, came together under the chairmanship of Robert Daly, Bishop of Cashel, to study prophecy. It seems probable that John Nelson Darby, more than any other of his day, was largely responsible for the revival of interest in eschatological teaching and also for the fresh realization of the significance of the dispensations. Dispensational teaching received a considerable impetus during the nineteenth century from the writings of J. N. Darby, Wm. Kelly, C. H. Mackintosh, W. E. Blackstone, W. Trotter, G. Campbell Morgan and others. Dr. G. Campbell Morgan's book, *God's Methods With Man,* published in 1898, provided a simple statement of the views of this school.

The popularization of the dispensational scheme of Biblical interpretation during the present century is due primarily to the *Scofield Reference Bible,* first published in 1909 under the editorship of Dr. C. I. Scofield, who was assisted by Dr. W. J. Erdman, Dr. A. C. Gaebelein, Dr. J. M. Gray, Dr. E. Harris, Prof. W. G. Moorehead, Dr. A. T.

Pierson and Dr. H. G. Weston. It should perhaps be emphasized that Scofield did not introduce any new scheme but merely applied what he had learned to the whole range of Scripture. Even the teachings of J. N. Darby, W. Kelly, etc., on this subject were very largely implicit in some of the interpretations propounded centuries before.

A more extreme view has been taken by ultradispensationalists such as Dr. E. W. Bullinger, well known for the erudition he has displayed in *The Companion Bible*, but this school has not found very wide support and seems to be dying out.

Possibly because of undue (and perhaps inappropriate) emphasis given by misguided teachers, there has of recent years been a violent reaction against the eschatological teachings of J. N. Darby and similar expositors and even more strongly against the implications of the dispensational structure of the *Scofield Bible*. In view of the extreme and injudicious statements made in some quarters, this attitude is not entirely unjustified. Even the use made of the word "dispensation" is not strictly accurate. The New Testament word *oikonomia* does not actually refer to an historical cycle but rather to a plan or stewardship. In his *Expository Dictionary of New Testament Words*, W. E. Vine says, "A dispensation is not a period or epoch (a common, but erroneous use of the word), but a mode of dealing, an arrangement, or administration of affairs." The use made of it has become so common, however, that it would be somewhat pedantic to suggest a substitute for it now.

If the subject is approached with an unprejudiced mind, the conclusion is inevitable that — by whatever name they may be called — there are certain clear divisions of history in the Bible and that, as a general rule, these are marked by God's promulgation of an appropriate covenant, defining His relationship with mankind and man's responsibilities to Him during that period. Any other conclusion creates difficulties of interpretation and results in questions which cannot be answered.

THE PERIOD OF INNOCENCE

Human history does not, of course, commence with the creation of the world, which may have taken place millennia ago, but with the creation of Adam and Eve. The Maker's work was perfect, and our first parents were found in a state of innocence and were placed in a perfect environment. Unhampered by the desires of a sinful nature and free from the shadows of pain, disease and trouble, these privileged souls might well have been expected to live in loyalty to their Creator, enjoying unbroken communion with Him and the unending bliss which He had made possible for them. They were given complete liberty, save for one prohibition. Of every tree of Eden's garden could they eat with the single exception of the tree of knowledge of good and evil (Genesis 2:17). By such a small test was their obedience to God to be proved. As one writer has said, the yoke thus laid upon them was not merely easy but well-nigh imperceptible, and only the distempered fancies of pride and self-will could have discovered any burden in it. They had been warned of the penalty attached to the contravention of God's command, but our two ancestors responded to temptation and fell, one sinning through pride and the other with deliberate intent. Even in ideal circumstances and in such privileged conditions, man proved incapable of retaining his innocence or fulfilling the will of God, and a righteous Creator had no alternative but to expel him from the earthly paradise. Thus sadly ended the first period of human probation.

THE RULE OF CONSCIENCE

God clothed His fallen creatures with skins (an early reminder that shelter and protection were now possible only through the sacrifice or death of another), and having disclosed the sorrows and hardships which must in the future condition human life, He set before them the hope of a future Redeemer (Genesis 3:14-19). Without law or government, man became responsible to abstain from evil and follow good, his guide being the dictates of his own conscience. Yet he had no innate goodness which led him to desire the right and possessed no inherent ability to overcome sin and thus enable him to observe the rule of conscience. The sixteen and one-half centuries of the antediluvian period are consequently a story of calamitous failure. The earth was filled with violence and corruption, and sin reigned over a guilty race. So awful were the conditions that God was compelled to sweep away the whole of mankind, with the exception of Noah and his family, by the judgment of the Flood (Genesis 7).

THE DISCIPLINE OF GOVERNMENT

In the post-diluvian world, the Almighty introduced a new principle by which the capacity of human nature for good was to be measured. Men were invested with the authority and responsibility for mutual self-government. The wrongdoer was to be punished for his crimes by his own fellows; the murderer, for example, was to pay with his own life for the life he had taken, and the sentence was to be executed by his fellow-men. The life of every individual was virtually in the care of those about him (Genesis 9:5, 6). Despite all the implications of the authority thus bestowed, Noah, who was the first to be so invested, was the first to reveal his inability even to govern himself (Genesis 9:21), and the incapacity he so quickly manifested was re-emphasized in his descendants. The only result of the new discipline was to create an ungodly solidarity of the race, which evidenced itself at Babel (Genesis 11:4). In the intoxication of their political union, men rebelled against

God and were only checked by His intervention and the judicial confusion of language. At the same time, as Pember remarks, "while their government served to unite them against their Creator, it utterly failed to restrain their moral corruption." Governmental responsibility still rests upon man's shoulders, but the dispensation which imposed it as a test concluded with his demonstrated failure.

THE PRINCIPLE OF FAITH

Through the period from Noah to Abraham, there had been, "a development of national pride, self-interest and consequent animosities," writes Campbell Morgan. "As a result, the solidarity of the race was lost, and a company of nations, with prejudices and pride, began to conflict with each other." In His divine wisdom, therefore, God chose the single family of Abraham for the purpose, "of creating a new nation, held together by the unifying principle of faith." He accordingly separated Abraham and his descendants from the other peoples of earth and pledged Himself to make of them a great nation, through whom all others should be blessed (Genesis 12:1-3). The Abrahamic covenant was unconditional, and its fulfillment depended, not upon man, but entirely upon the faithfulness of God; consequently its promises must one day come to fruition. The dispensation during which the covenant was given, however, was another period of divine testing — this time on a completely different basis from any previously. The result was the same. Unwilling to exercise implicit faith and trust in God, Abraham's descendants eventually found themselves in miserable servitude in Egypt, and even when God had mercifully delivered them, they heedlessly surrendered His promises for the bondage of the law (Exodus 19:8). Having experienced divine grace, they despised the goodness of God and accepted Sinai's binding legality in lieu. The dispensation came to an end through their own action, but by that very fact, they testified clearly to their own failure.

THE AGE OF LAW

With the giving of the law, a new era began, and until the first advent of the Lord Jesus Christ, Israel was measured by the standard they had so readily accepted. There could be no dubiety about Jehovah's requirements. Divine regulations were given for almost every detail of the national and individual life. Sacrifices, offerings, festivals, priesthood, social conduct and relationships, sanitary questions, etc., were all governed by God-given rules. But the history of the nation under prophet, priest and king, demonstrated the people's failure to fulfill God's will, and Stephen's final charge in this respect was that they had, "received the law by the disposition of angels and have not kept it." Indeed, they added to their transgression, for they rejected the theocracy and demanded a monarchy. Having secured their desire, they were split into two because of discontent, and both of the resultant kingdoms proved so incorrigibly evil that they were punished by removal from the land. Even when a remnant was permitted to return, they substituted formalism for spirituality and indifference for sincerity; observance of the law was in the letter rather than the spirit. Finally, when their true Messiah came, they rejected Him and gave conclusive proof of their iniquity at Calvary. God thereupon cast them out of their land and rejected them as His people.

THE PARENTHESIS OF GRACE

After the death of Christ, God set aside the nation of Israel and, in the words of the Jerusalem council, "did visit the Gentiles, to take out of them a people for His name" (Acts 15:14). During this age, individuals are regenerated by the Holy Spirit and united to the living Christ. They have a heavenly citizenship, and all their prospects are heavenly and not earthly. The present age is one of grace (Titus 3:4, 5) and salvation is dependent upon acceptance or rejection of Christ, but as Scofield remarks, "The predicted end of the testing of man under grace is the apostasy of the professing church." The majority of the world treat God's proffered grace with either apathetic indifference or bitter opposition, and relatively few respond to the offer of mercy and salvation in Christ. The church which assumes His name is unfaithful to Him, and the apocalyptic seer vividly describes her last state as "the mother of harlots" (Revelation 17). So completely will man's failure be demonstrated even during a period of super-abounding grace, and our Lord will bring the age to a conclusion by removing the true church (I Thessalonians 4:15-17).

THE REIGN OF RIGHTEOUSNESS

The prophetic Scriptures make it clear that, before the seventh dispensation is ushered in with the resumption of God's relationship with Israel and the revelation of our Lord in His glory, the earth is to pass through a period of unparalleled tribulation. The world which rejected Christ will bow to Antichrist, and the nation which refused its rightful Messiah will be subjected to the rule of a devil-inspired king. At the appointed time, however, the Lord Jesus Christ will return to earth to establish His long-promised kingdom (Daniel 2:44) and to enter into a new covenant with His people (Jeremiah 31:31-34). Satan will be cast into the abyss, and for a thousand years Christ will reign over the earth in righteousness and equity. Israel will be set at the head of the nations; the groaning creation will be delivered from its thraldom; oppression and suffering will be banished; and longevity will be universal. Man will be tried under the most favourable conditions possible but only to prove his complete depravity, for the dispensation will end in a universal revolt resultant from the release of Satan from the pit (Revelation 20:7-9). As in every dispensation, man's failure will be followed by the judgment of God, and fire from heaven will consume the rebels.

THE LAST ASSIZE

Whatever the dispensation and whatever the method of testing divinely adopted, man proves himself to be hopelessly and unalterably sinful. He is never able to attain the standard of divine requirements and, apart from the grace of God, could contemplate only ruin as his prospect. By grace alone is he delivered from the shackles of his own sinfulness and brought into a relationship with God Himself. But for the unregenerate man there is no hope. The seer in the Revelation foretells the dissolution of heaven and earth (cf. II Peter 3:10-12) and then depicts a great white throne, suspended in space, before which are summoned the dead, to be "judged out of those things which were written in the books . . . and whosoever was not found written in the book of life was cast into the lake of fire" (Revelation 20:12-15). At this final assize the sinner will himself be convinced of his sin and will forever be banished from the presence of God.

THE ETERNAL STATE

The apostle declares that, after the millennial reign of Christ, there "cometh the end, when He shall have delivered up the kingdom to God, even the Father when He shall have put down all rule and all authority and power" (I Corinthians 15:24). Some writers have deduced from this that before the handing over of authority to the Father, a further age is to follow the millennium, in which the Old Testament prophecies shall be fulfilled and lasting happiness shall be the lot of the King's subjects. When dispensations pass away, however, there are to be new heavens and a new earth in place of those destroyed by fire; the presence of God will be known among men; the divine glory will be unveiled to His creatures; and the eternal throne will apparently be visible to mortal eyes (Revelation 21:22). What the ultimate future holds in detail is not disclosed, and it is indeed beyond the comprehension of man. But it is clear that the One who sees the end from the beginning has from the commencement unmistakably been directing His program towards that end and that His hand has been manifest throughout the whole history of the human race. When dispensations finally disappear, He will still abide.

THE TIMES OF THE GENTILES

Overlapping the dispensations is another period, referred to in the New Testament as "the times of the Gentiles". In His prediction of the destruction of Jerusalem by the Romans, our Lord declared, ". . . Jerusalem shall be trodden down by the Gentiles, until the times of the Gentiles be fulfilled" (Luke 21:24). Subsequently, the apostle Paul said, ". . . blindness in part is happened to Israel, until the fulness of the Gentiles be come in" (Romans 11:25).

Centuries earlier, the inveterate sin and idolatry of Israel and later of Judah led to God's rejection of His people and to their removal from their own land to Assyria (II Kings 17:18-23), and Chaldea (II Kings 24:14; 25:21). The full weight of the long-threatened chastisement for wrongdoing (Leviticus 26) did not fall upon the nation immediately, and the additional judgment foretold by our Lord in Luke 21:24 was not meted out until the Jews had filled up the measure of their guilt by killing the Prince of life. The condign punishment consequently experienced has justly continued to the present day.

Following upon God's repudiation of the people, governmental supremacy in the earth was Divinely bestowed upon Gentile powers, commencing with the Babylonian empire and its autocratic ruler, Nebuchadnezzar (Daniel 2:37, 38). Gentile rule has held sway ever since and, as Daniel clearly indicates, will continue to be exercised until the establishment of the kingdom of God upon earth (Daniel 2:44; 7: 13, 14). This period of "the times of the Gentiles" has already lasted nearly two and a half millennia. At present,* the old city of Jerusalem, including the site of the former temple, is firmly held by the Hashemite Kingdom of Jordan; it is still "trodden down of the Gentiles." (The Israeli city of Jerusalem is almost entirely a new town built by the Jews during the present century.) Furthermore, the apostle John refers to the holy city yet being trodden under foot by the Gentiles for forty-two months (Revelation 11:2), i.e. for the latter half of the seventieth "week" of Daniel 9:27. For the centuries of Gentile rule, Israel has ceased to be recognized by God, and His ultimate purposes of blessing for her have been held in abeyance. Dr. H. Grattan Guinness has pertinently written in *Light for the Last Days,* "The times of the Gentiles are marked by Jewish loss of dominion and independence, by Jewish subjection to and suffering under Gentile conquerors, by the dispersion of the twelve tribes of Israel, and by the subjection of their land." World empires have risen and fallen, but the times of the Gentiles continue. Although ingenious attempts have been made to calculate the length of this period, they have been based upon false premises, and there is no Biblical revelation of its precise duration.

At present, Israel as a nation is blind to the revelation of God in Christ and to the truth of His grace (II Corinthians 3:14; Romans 11:25), and Divine blessing has reached out instead to the Gentiles (Romans 15:16). There is no distinction of race in the Church, however, and many individual Jews during the last nineteen centuries have accepted Christ as their Saviour in the same way as individual Gentiles — a number whom Paul describes as ". . . a remnant according to the election of grace" (Romans 11:5) — but on the other hand, the characteristic feature of the present age is that God is now calling out a people for Himself from the Gentiles (Acts 15:14). This operation will, of course, finish with the completion of the Church, when "the fullness of the Gentiles" will have "come in". With the removal of the

*In June, 1967, the Israelis regained possession of old Jerusalem.

church at the rapture, a reawakened Israel will then turn to the One Who comes out of Zion to deliver His people and to purge their ungodliness (Romans 11:26).

The long period of the times of the Gentiles will conclude with the judgment of the Gentile nations at our Lord's return in glory to this earth (Matthew 25:31-46). Gentile domination will then be broken, Jerusalem will again be free and a restored Israel will experience the beneficent reign of its long-expected Messiah. The period is not synchronous with any of the dispensations as such, and it clearly overlaps at least two of the dispensations and runs up to the commencement of the golden age of the millennium.

CHAPTER III. # Israel, Jehovah's People

WHEN GOD called out Abraham from Ur of the Chaldees (Genesis 11:31), it was with the object of creating a new nation which was distinct from all others — a people who were holy and a special possession to Him (Deuteronomy 7:6), an elect race. Balaam subsequently declared, ". . . the people shall dwell alone, and shall not be reckoned among the nations" (Numbers 23:9). It was the Divine intention that this new nation of Israel should be a pure theocracy and, as Edersheim says, "Not only in its ecclesiastical, but in its political constitution also, was it to show forth the supremacy, the authority, and the continued presence of Jehovah." In the midst of a corrupt and idolatrous world, Israel, as a sanctified nation, was to demonstrate her loyalty and faithfulness to the One who had separated her to Himself. She was God's chosen people, upon whom His love was arbitrarily set and on behalf of whom His saving power had been exercised (Deuteronomy 7:8; Isaiah 43:3, 4; Malachi 1:2).

God made certain pledges to them in respect of their future blessing. He bound Himself to Abraham by an unconditional covenant of such importance that He declared it in various forms ten times — six times to Abraham and two each to Isaac and Jacob (Genesis 12:1-3; 13:14-17; 15:1-7; 17:1-18; etc.). In addition to the Divine promises to Abraham personally, blessing was promised to his seed, who were likened to the stars of heaven (Genesis 15:5), to the sand on the seashore (Genesis 22:17) and to the dust of the earth (Genesis 13:16), so countless in numbers were they to be. There was, of course, an implication in the symbols that the patriarch would have a spiritual posterity (innumerable as the stars) as well as a physical posterity (numberless as the grains of sand and dust), and it is significant that some of the blessings covenanted were spiritual and others material. Prof. J. F. Walvoord in *The Millennial Kingdom* concisely summarizes the promises to Abraham's seed, "The nation itself shall be great (Genesis 12:2) and innumerable (Genesis 13:16). The nation is promised possession of the land. Its extensive boundaries are given in detail (Genesis 15:18-21). In connection with the promise of the land, the Abrahamic covenant itself is expressly called 'everlasting' (Genesis 17:7) and the possession of the land is defined as 'an everlasting possession' (Genesis 17:8). It should be immediately clear that this promise guarantees both the everlasting continuance of the seed as a nation and its everlasting possession of the land."

The covenant was unconditional for Abraham and was binding only upon God. No provision was made for its revocation, and it cannot, therefore, be annulled. Indeed, in Galatians 3:17, the apostle Paul argues emphatically that the Mosaic law, given 430 years later, cannot abrogate the provisions of the covenant. The promises must be fulfilled, and Israel is guaranteed an everlasting continuance as a nation with everlasting possession of the promised land. Lest it should be argued that Israel's sin had broken the covenant, the apostle shows clearly in Romans 11 that God has not cast off Israel and that the nation's present blindness will exist only until the completion of the fulness of the Gentiles (v. 25). In Isaiah 54:10, God declared that the mountains should depart and the hills be removed, but that His covenant with Israel should not be removed. In Jeremiah 31:35, 36, He declared that only if the sun, moon and stars departed, would Israel cease to be a nation. Ezekiel 37:25-28 plainly states, "And they shall dwell in the land that I have given unto Jacob, my servant," and that this shall be for ever; God Himself will dwell in the midst of them and will sanctify His people. The covenant is binding and permanent.

In so blessing Israel, God's purpose was that the people should be a constant witness to Him among the nations surrounding them, but it was just here that she failed. "Israel was created to influence other nations for God," wrote Dr. Campbell Morgan, "but she rebelled against God's rule and ended in Egypt and slavery." Nevertheless, He afforded them a further opportunity, and four centuries later they were Divinely delivered and eventually brought into the promised land of Canaan. After the exodus from Egypt they accepted the Mosaic law and came under the specific rule of God. The people soon wearied of theocracy, however, and demanded a monarchy like all other nations (I Samuel 8:5). Despite their implicit rejection of Him, God graciously granted them their desire, but it was not until Solomon came to the throne that the regal splendour they craved for was realized, although at a higher price than they had envisaged. The introduction of foreign luxury and foreign customs gradually resulted, as one writer says, in a "corruption of the social and religious life of the nation", and "from that period we may date the commencement of the peculiar pre-Babylonian form of religious apostasy."

When David was established on his throne, God entered into a covenant with him, promising that his house, his throne and his kingdom should be established for ever (II Samuel 7:12-16). As in the case of the Abrahamic covenant, no conditions were imposed on the beneficiary; it was an unconditional covenant, binding only upon God. It was quite irrevocable, and in Psalm 89:28, 29, 34-37 He declared that His covenant with David should not be broken, that

David's seed should endure for ever and his throne should be as permanent as the sun. Jeremiah 33:20-26 expressed it equally plainly: only if day and night ceased to be would the covenant with David be broken or his seed disowned. Isaiah 54:8-10 provides further confirmation: mountains and hills would be displaced before the Davidic covenant was disturbed. The covenant was an everlasting one (Ezekiel 37:26). Israel's transgressions could not annul an irrevocable covenant. Moral failure may result in punishment, but it cannot frustrate the Divine purposes or permanently alienate God's people from Him. The covenants defined His relationship to Israel and detailed His intention to bless the nation. He will never repudiate His pledges; He must fulfill His word. Just as a wayward child remains the child of its parents, so a disobedient Israel retains her relationship to Jehovah. His purposes depend upon Himself and not upon the fidelity of His people. "The gifts and calling of God are without repentance" (Romans 11:29).

On the death of Solomon, the kingdom was divided into two, ten tribes crowning Jeroboam the son of Nebat as king while the other two tribes retained their loyalty to Rehoboam, Solomon's son (I Kings 12). The two kingdoms continued side by side until 721 B.C., when as a result of the sin of the northern kingdom of Israel, the people were carried away captive by the Assyrians (II Kings 17:5, 6). The lesson made little impression on the southern kingdom of Judah, and in 598 B.C., the king and the chief people were carried into captivity by Nebuchadnezzar, and nine years later most of those who remained were transported to Babylon (II Kings 24:11-17; 25:1-11). Although some of the exiles were subsequently allowed to return (Ezra 2:1), the land of Israel has been under Gentile domination ever since, and our Lord indicated that this would continue "until the times of the Gentiles be fulfilled" (Luke 21:24). Chaldea, Medo-Persia, Greece and Rome have successively held the land in sway; Saracen, Turk and Briton have made their rule felt; and even today the Jordanian Arab controls some of the country. The ancient city of Jerusalem (as distinct from the Jewish modern city) is still "trodden down of the Gentiles".

It was during the Roman regime that one of heaven's eternal purposes was fulfilled, and the Messiah was born of Israel. But "He came unto His own, and His own received Him not" (John 1:11). He declared that He was sent only to "the lost sheep of the house of Israel" (Matthew 15:24) and that "salvation is of the Jews" (John 4:22). Yet His message was ignored, and the Messiah was rejected. The One so long foretold by prophet and seer, the One for whom Israel impatiently waited, had come, but they were deaf to His voice and blind to His claims, and eventually the Hope of Israel was delivered into the hands of the Gentiles to be crucified. The long-promised kingdom had been offered and rejected. "It cannot be denied", says G. E. Ladd in *The Gospel of the Kingdom*, "that Jesus offered the kingdom to Israel. When He sent His disciples upon their preaching mission, He told them not to go among the Gentiles, but to 'go rather to the lost sheep of the house of Israel' (Matthew 10:6). Jesus rebuffed a Canaanitish woman with the words, 'I was sent only to the lost sheep of the house of Israel' (Matthew 15:24). Furthermore, our Lord spoke of the Jews as the 'sons of the kingdom' (Matthew 8:12), even though they were rejecting the Messiah and the kingdom of God. They were the sons of the kingdom because it was Israel whom God had chosen and to whom He had promised the blessings of the kingdom. The kingdom was theirs by right of election, history and heritage. So it was that our Lord directed His ministry to them and offered to them that which had been promised them."

Our Lord made clear the consequences of their rejection when He declared, "the kingdom of God shall be taken from you" (Matthew 21:43). Although the mercy of God still reaches the individual Jew who puts His trust in Christ, the nation has been temporarily set aside and judicially blinded until the purposes of God for the Gentiles have been fulfilled (Romans 11:8, 25). God has not permanently cast off His people (Romans 11:26), but their rejection of the Messiah resulted in a severance of their national relationship with Jehovah (as predicted in Hosea's domestic experiences centuries earlier). Through Israel's unbelief and consequent fall, blessing has become available to others. But it seems clear that Divine mercy will one day restore the nation to favour again (Romans 11:24).

It is sometimes taught that the elect remnant of Israel, who accepted the gospel and were incorporated with Gentile believers into the one body of the Church, became the "holy nation" of I Peter 2:9 and that this was the "direct and plenary fulfillment of the assurances given in the Old Testament that Israel was not to cease from being a nation before the Lord for ever." But this virtually implies that Israel *has*, in fact, ceased from being a nation and has been superseded by the Church, the latter thus becoming the inheritor of all the promises to Israel. The blessings of this age, however, as another has pointed out, "do not correspond with the predictions of the restoration and conversion of Israel, with the predictions of Israel's supremacy on a regenerated earth (Isaiah 14:1-3; 41:11, 12; 49:22-26; 51:22, 23; 54:17; 60:12, 14, 16), or with the return of fertility to Canaan (Isaiah 35:7; 41:18, 19; 43:20; 55:12, 13; 60:13; Jeremiah 31:5)." The only conclusion which can be reached is that the covenants made with Israel still await fulfillment.

At the Jerusalem conference referred to in Acts 15, James declared that after God had taken a people out of the Gentiles, He would return and rebuild the fallen tabernacle of David (Acts 15:13-18). James was, of course, quoting Amos 9:11, 12, where the prophet depicted the fortunes of Israel as a fallen tabernacle and indicated quite clearly that when the times of the Gentiles have run their course and when the church is complete, it is God's intention to turn again to His earthly people of Israel. To use the apostle Paul's metaphor in Romans 11:24, the natural branch, which was broken off, is to be grafted back into the olive tree.

Israel's rejection of her Messiah led to Jerusalem being "trodden down of the Gentiles". For the last nineteen centuries God, having set Israel aside, has been forming the church — a heavenly and not an earthly people. But there are not wanting indications that the church age is reaching its end, and that soon all believers in Christ will be removed from this earth at His descent to the air. When that happens, James' prediction will be fulfilled, and God will resume His relationship with Israel.

There must be a future repatriation of Israel if a land co-terminous with the promised boundaries is to be their inalienable possession and if the royal house is to be established in perpetuity. There can be no dubiety about the Divine purpose. God declared, "In a little wrath I hid my face from thee for a moment, but with everlasting kindness will I have mercy on thee, saith the Lord thy Redeemer. For this is as the waters of Noah unto me; for as I have sworn that the waters of Noah should no more go over the earth; so I have sworn that I would not be wroth with thee, nor rebuke thee. For the mountains shall depart, and the hills be removed; but My kindness shall not depart from thee, neither shall the covenant of my peace be removed, saith the Lord, who hath mercy upon thee" (Isaiah 54:8-10). If this is not sufficiently explicit, Jeremiah records the words of the Lord, ". . . who giveth the sun for a light by day, and the ordinances of the moon and of the stars for a light by night, who divideth the sea when the waves thereof roar. . . . If those ordinances depart from before me, saith the Lord, then the seed of Israel also shall cease from being a nation before Me for ever" (Jeremiah 31:35, 36). Sun, moon and stars must disappear before Israel loses her national position. Equally emphatic is the assurance given by

Ezekiel, "they shall dwell in the land that I have given unto Jacob, my servant, in which your fathers have dwelt; and they shall dwell therein, even they, and their children, and their children's children for ever: and My servant, David, shall be their prince for ever. Moreover, I will make a covenant of peace with them; it shall be an everlasting covenant with them; and I will place them, and multiply them, and will set My sanctuary in the midst of them for evermore" (Ezekiel 37:25, 26). Nothing could be clearer than the Scriptural statements of the Divine purpose.

The Old Testament prophets repeatedly and explicitly foretell the restoration of Israel. Jeremiah declares that God will cause the captivity of Judah and Israel to return and that He will build them again as at the first (Jeremiah 37:7, 8). Ezekiel states that, for His name's sake, God will gather His people out of the nations and bring them into their own land (Ezekiel 36:22-24). Hosea says, "Israel shall abide many days without a king, and without a prince, and without a sacrifice . . . afterwards shall the children of Israel return and seek the Lord their God, and David their king" (Hosea 3:4, 5). Lest there should be any doubt, Ezekiel reveals that the two kingdoms of Israel and Judah are to be re-united and to be reconstituted as one nation (Ezekiel 37:16-22). The details are quite plain, and God must fulfil His word. "The gifts and calling of God are without repentance," declared the apostle Paul (Romans 11:29), and what God has promised He will perform. "Like as I have brought all this great evil upon this people," He said, "so I will bring upon them all the good that I have promised them" (Jeremiah 32:42).

If, as we believe, the seventieth "week" of Daniel 9:27 is still unfulfilled, it is essential for Israel to be in her own land in order that the western powers may enter into the predicted treaty with her. Similarly, a returned Israel and a rebuilt temple are essential for the fulfillment of II Thessalonians 2:2-4, and Matthew 24:15-31 and other Scriptures.

For these events to happen, the elect of the present day (i.e. the church) must first be removed, but present conditions suggest that this is not far distant.

It is clear from our Lord's own words, as well as from Old Testament prophecy, that the prospect before the restored Jew is first a period of unparalleled tribulation and judgment, which will be brought to an end by the return of the Lord to the earth to set up the kingdom for which Israel has been waiting. In that day, the unfulfilled prophecies of a glorious reign in which there will be peace, righteousness and equity will come to fruition, and the age-long pledges of the land as an everlasting possession will be implemented. Even the tribal boundaries of Ezekiel 47 and 48 have yet to be realized, and there can be no doubt that there is a future for the nation.

There can be no possibility of interpreting prophecies such as Isaiah 11:6-10 and 65:19-25 otherwise than literally, and any attempt to spiritualize them and make them applicable to the Church is ill-reasoned. "Hath God cast away His people?" asked the apostle Paul. "God hath not cast away His people which He foreknew" (Romans 11:1, 2).

 # Daniel's Seventy Weeks

WHEN THE seventy years of Judah's servitude to Babylon foretold by Jeremiah (Jeremiah 25:11, 12; 29:10-14; see also II Chronicles 36:19-21) had nearly expired, it was revealed to the later prophet Daniel that a further period of "seventy weeks" was decreed upon his people (the Jews) and upon His holy city (Jerusalem). In his prayer preceding the revelation, Daniel had referred to the people and the city as God's. The fact that Gabriel described them as Daniel's is an indication that they were not fully acknowledged by God in the restoration under Zerubbabel which subsequently took place; they still remained under Gentile sovereignty. When "the times of the Gentiles" are fulfilled, God will, of course, effect a second restoration, and the Jews will then be recognized as His people and the city will be built to Him (Isaiah 11:11; Jeremiah 31:31-40).

There has been considerable controversy regarding the meaning of the word *shabua*, translated "weeks" in Daniel 9, but most competent Hebraists agree that it is a generic term, simply meaning "sevens", without indicating any particular denomination of time, such as days or years. That the heptads or hepdomads of Daniel 9 were years, however, seems fairly clear. The same word is translated "seven years", for example, in Joseph's interpretation of Pharaoh's dream (Genesis 41:26), and it is also used in the Mishna and in the book of Jubilees for "weeks" of years. Dr. S. P. Tregelles writes, "Daniel has made enquiry about seventy *years* of captivity in Babylon. The answer speaks also of seventy periods, which in our English translation are called weeks. The word, however, does not necessarily mean seven *days,* but *a period of seven parts;* of course, it is much more often used in speaking of a week than anything else, because nothing is so often mentioned as a week which is similarly divided. The Hebrews, however, used a septenary scale as to time just as habitually as we should reckon tens; the sabbatical years, the jubilees, all tended to give this thought a permanent place in their minds. The denomination is here to be taken from the subject of Daniel's prayer. He prayed about years; he is answered about periods of seven years, i.e. the recurrence of sabbatical years." The period referred to in Daniel 9 was seventy heptads of years or 490 years.

The year of the prophecy was not, of course, the equivalent of twelve months of the Gregorian calendar. Both in Babylonian and Jewish reckoning the year was a lunisolar one of 360 days. As far back as in the days of Noah, the year was reckoned as 360 days, and a month as thirty days; for example, after the flood the number of days in the five months from the seventeenth day of the second month to the seventeenth day of the seventh month was stated to be 150 days (Genesis 7:11; 8:3, 4). "All nations before the just length of the solar year was known," says Sir Isaac Newton, "reckoned months by the course of the moon, and years by the return of winter and summer, spring and autumn; and in making calendars for their festivals, they reckoned thirty days to a lunar month, and twelve lunar months to a year, taking the nearest round numbers, whence came the division of the ecliptic into 360 degrees." In Revelation 11:2, 3, a period of forty-two months is subsequently described as 1,260 days, which again confirms that a month was reckoned as thirty days.

The 490 years decreed upon Daniel's people and his holy city of Jerusalem were to see the fulfillment of certain purposes of God. Six were specifically detailed.

(1) "To finish the transgression." The word *kata*, translated "finish", means to shut up or restrain from a course of activity, and the word *pesha*, translated "transgression", means a defection, revolt or rebellion. Israel's lawbreaking seemed to be completely unrestrained. For their rebellion against God, they had been delivered into captivity, but this experience had taught them no lesson, and nothing apparently held their deliberate willfulness in check. Their rebellion was to be finished, however. As N. C. Deck points out, when He makes "a new covenant with the house of Judah and Israel, God will put His law in their inward parts, and write it on their hearts, and then they will have an inward restraint." Their rebellion will effectually finish at the return of Messiah to earth.

(2) "To make an end of sins." The nation's wrongdoing will be brought to a definite end. When Christ returns, ". . . the iniquity of Israel shall be sought for, and there shall be none; and the sins of Judah, and they shall not be found. . . ." (Jeremiah 50:20). The expression employed in Daniel 9:24, according to Cooper, was consistently "used to indicate the closing of a letter or official document. When the scribe had finished his work, the king placed his royal seal upon it, thus showing that the communication was brought to a close and, at the same time, giving it the official imprimatur. The primary idea is that of bringing a matter to a conclusion."

(3) "To make reconciliation for iniquity." Acts of wrongdoing might come to an end under the restrictive hand of God, but the sinful tendency of the individual would not be changed thereby, nor would he be freed from the guilt of past trespasses. Atonement and reconciliation were necessary if the estranged nation and individual were to be brought back to God. Guilt must be removed and

sins forgiven. Although the basis for this was laid at the Cross, its effect will be experienced only when the nation looks upon the One whom they pierced and mourns repentantly for Him (Zechariah 12:10).

(4) "To bring in the righteousness of the ages." The nation is to be regenerated (Ezekiel 36:24-27), and God says that then, "I bring near my righteousness . . . and I will place salvation in Zion for Israel my glory" (Isaiah 46:13). Righteousness will be introduced by the Messiah, and in His millennial kingdom, of which Daniel thus caught a glimpse, there will be a rule of righteousness and equity.

(5) "To seal up vision and prophecy." When Messiah's kingdom is set up, there will be no more need for vision or prophecy; all will have been fulfilled. The affixing of a seal is an indication that, prophecy having been fulfilled, no further prophetic activity was necessary.

(6) "To anoint a most holy." Many expositors assume that this refers to our Lord's anointing with the Holy Spirit at His baptism (Acts 10:37, 38), but the words "most holy" are consistently used of objects, such as the temple and its inmost sanctuary, the temple vessels, the incense, etc.; the expression is never applied to persons in the Old Testament. Solomon's temple was filled with the shekinah glory (I Kings 8:11) but, prior to the destruction of the building, the glory was withdrawn (Ezekiel 10:18, 19; 11:23). In the millennial temple, the glory of God will again be present (Ezekiel 43:1-5), and it is doubtless to this consecration of the temple, not by literal anointing with oil but by the presence of the shekinah, that Gabriel alluded. All of these six blessings plainly still lie in the future since Israel is still suffering for her sins and the kingdom has not yet been established.

The seventy weeks of the prophecy were to commence with the issuing of a command to restore and build Jerusalem, and this commencing date must clearly be determined first if the prophecy is to be correctly interpreted.

There are several dates which expositors consider as possible starting points. In Ezra 1:1-3, for example, mention is made of a proclamation by Cyrus, the Emperor of Persia, authorizing, *inter alia,* the rebuilding of the temple but making no reference to the city itself. A decree was subsequently issued by Darius confirming that of Cyrus (Ezra 6:1-12) but again making no mention of the city. Again, the historian records that a royal letter regarding the temple (but saying nothing of the city) was given to Ezra by Artaxerxes (Ezra 7:11-26). It is clear that none of these can be regarded as the point from which the seventy weeks commenced. But in 445 B.C. Artaxerxes explicitly authorized Nehemiah to rebuild the city (Nehemiah 2:5-9): this alone can be regarded then as the commencing date.

The period of seventy weeks was divided into three sections of seven weeks (or forty-nine years), sixty-two weeks (or 434 years) and one week (or seven years). The first forty-nine years were to be occupied in the building of the city. During that time the broad plaza or square (the center of the life of the city) and the scarped rampart or wall (rather than "moat" as in the A.V.) were to be rebuilt, i.e., by implication not merely the center and circumference, but the whole of the city. The rebuilding was to be in troublous times, and the Scriptures (Nehemiah 4:1-14; 6:1-14, 9:36, 37) indicate the difficulties experienced at this particular period. Forty-nine years from Nehemiah 2 carry us to the date of Malachi's prophecy, and it is not without significance that his book closed the Old Testament canon.

The second section of 434 years ran from the expiration of the first forty-nine years "unto the Anointed One, the Prince." In *Daniel in the Critic's Den,* Sir Robert Anderson has argued (after converting the 483 lunisolar years into Julian years) that this period expired on the day on which our Lord rode into Jerusalem (Matthew 21:1-11) in fulfillment of Zechariah's prophecy (Zechariah 9:9). Without necessarily accepting his statement that the edict of Artaxerxes was issued on the first day of Nisan, 445 B.C., it was certainly in that month (Nehemiah 2:1), and it could scarcely have been much later than the first day in view of subsequent events detailed in the prophecy.

After (the word used is *achar*, which usually means immediately after — see Genesis 5:4; 41:29, 30; Ezekiel 40: 1), the sixty-ninth week (or 483rd year), Messiah, the Anointed One, was to be cut off and have nothing (by implication, no posterity). The word translated "cut off" is that normally used of the death penalty (Leviticus 7:20) inflicted by a judge or court of judicature and usually implies a violent death even when otherwise used (cf. Psalm 37:9). In fulfillment of the prophecy, when the sixty-ninth week had run its course, our Lord was "cut off out of the land of the living" and no posterity was left to Him (Isaiah 53:8).

Following the crucifixion of Christ, retribution was to overtake the guilty nation of Israel; according to Daniel's prophecy, "the people of the coming prince shall destroy the city and the sanctuary" (i.e. Jerusalem and the temple) and war should continue to the end, since desolations had been determined by God. The prediction was completely fulfilled in 70 A.D., when the city and the temple were destroyed by the Romans. Since the destroyers were Romans, it is evident that "the coming prince" (who has still not yet appeared) must originate in the area of the Roman Empire too.

This prince is to make a covenant (presumably that of Isaiah 28:15-18) with the many of Israel for a period of one week — patently the last of the seventy weeks. It is sometimes argued that it is the Messiah who is to make the covenant, but the coming prince is a nearer antecedent to the "he" of Daniel 9:27 than the Messiah. In any case, Messiah's covenant will not be restricted to seven years but will be an everlasting one. It is equally clear that the new covenant of Jeremiah 31:31-40 is not in view; that will be made with Israel at Messiah's return to earth. The covenant will obviously be a seven years' treaty entered into by a ruler arising out of the area of the former Roman Empire.

This treaty has not yet been enacted, and the only possible conclusion is that the events of the seventieth week have yet to be fulfilled, and that a parenthesis (which has already lasted over nineteen centuries) has been interposed. Daniel gave a plain hint of this parenthesis since, as G. H. Pember pertinently remarks, he "placed events between the sixty-ninth and the seventieth seven, namely, the death of the Lord Jesus, the destruction of Jerusalem and the temple forty years later, and a continuance of war 'until the end' of the age. It is only after the words 'until the end' that he introduced the last seven. Thus he clearly intimated that there would be an interval between the sixty-ninth and seventieth sevens and that it would be protracted until the time of the end." Pember also points out, "in each of the great prophecies of Moses (Leviticus 26; Deuteronomy 28: 30, 32), it was predicted that the Jews must be driven out of their country and scattered among all nations for a long exile, during which God would suspend His dealings with them and no longer recognize them as His people. This period of non-recognition is manifestly the same as the interval between the sixty-ninth and the seventieth seven." That divine calculations ignore periods of time during which God has chastised His people by delivering them into servitude, may be deduced from many Scriptures. For instance, I Kings 6:1 states that Solomon began to build the temple 480 years after the Exodus, but a simple calculation shows that it was 594 years and not 480, the balance of 114 years being accounted for by the 111 years of servitude and the three years of Abimelech's usurpation referred to in the book of Judges.

The Scriptures contain many instances of parentheses which are not at first apparent. Many expositors believe, for example, that there is a gap in time (possibly of several millennia) between verses 1 and 2 of Genesis 1, while the rule of Christ referred to in the latter part of Isaiah 9:6 is also separated by nearly 2,000 years at least from the birth mentioned in the first clause of the same verse. Again, when our Lord took the roll to read in the synagogue at Nazareth (Luke 4:16-20), He stopped abruptly in the middle of Isaiah 61:2, intimating plainly that the latter part of the verse was not then to be fulfilled but related to a later time. There was a hiatus between verses 9 and 10 of Zechariah 9, since the first verse was plainly fulfilled at our Lord's entry into Jerusalem (Matthew 21:5-9), whereas verse 10 is still unfulfilled nineteen centuries later. Once more, Luke 1:31 was fulfilled at our Lord's birth, but verses 32 and 33 still await fulfillment. A simliar break is found between verses 5 and 6 of Revelation 12. The illustrations might be multiplied, but probably sufficient has been said to show that parentheses of the kind found in Daniel 9 are not uncommon.

The sin of Israel culminated in the rejection and murder of their Messiah, and God accordingly set aside the nation (Romans 11:11, 15, 25) and commenced to deal with individuals of every race and nationality. Since Israel has apostasized from Him, He ceased to take account of time in relation to them, and the seventieth week of Daniel 9 has consequently not yet commenced. In the meantime, God is calling out a people to form a church — a mystery hidden until the revelation made through the apostle Paul in New Testament days (Ephesians 3:3-11) — and not until that work is complete will He resume His relationship with Israel. When the church has been removed from the scene (I Thessalonians 4:14-17), however, time will again start to be measured.

In other words, the present dispensation must be complete and the church must have been removed before it is possible for the seventieth week of Daniel 9 to commence. Norman Deck pertinently remarks, "At the present time, the Jews are on a parity with the Gentiles as regards the gospel, rather than having a position of privilege over them. Now God cannot act towards the Jews on two incompatible principles at the same time, that is to say, He cannot treat the Jews on a priority basis over the Gentiles, and on a parity basis with them, *at the same time.* Now since the nation Israel did possess a position of privilege over the Gentiles during the sixty-nine weeks which terminated at the Crucifixion, but forfeited that position by that act, which forfeiture has continued during the present parenthesis, it surely follows that, when the seventieth week takes up its running (it being of the same nature as the sixty-nine weeks), this position of privilege will be restored to that race on the ground of a godly remnant who will be converted to God at that time (probably on account of the shock of the rapture of the Church and through the preaching of the 'two witnesses' of Revelation 11:3-11), and who will remain loyal to their coming Messiah in spite of having to endure extreme persecution from the Man of Sin. But while the church is still on the earth, the Jewish race can enjoy no such privilege. It is submitted, therefore, that the church must be off the scene before the seventieth week starts."

It is clear from Daniel 2 and 7 that, before the return of Christ to set up His kingdom, a federation of powers is to come into being, and this is confirmed in Revelation 13 and 17. The details furnished by John in the last book of the Bible reveal that the federation will be dominated by a ruthless and despotic individual whom the apostle termed "the beast". This latter-day ruler of the revived Roman Empire seems undoubtedly the man described by Gabriel as "the coming prince" (Daniel 9:26). It is this one who will make the seven year treaty with Israel of which Daniel spoke and which synchronizes with the seventieth week.

The purpose of the covenant is not explicitly stated, but it seems evident from Isaiah 28 that one of its provisions will be the protection of Israel from invasion by the Assyrian or "king of the north." It will be ineffective, however, for the Assyrian is the rod of God's anger, sent by Him against an impious nation (Isaiah 10:5, 6), and the protection of the western powers will be unavailing against the northern invader; carnage and desolation will tell the story of his passage through the land (Psalm 74 etc.).

Halfway through the term of the covenant, the Roman prince will put a stop to the offering of sacrifices by the Jews (Daniel 9:27), and, as II Thessalonians 2:3, 4 indicates, will defile the temple by idolatry. There is an implication in Daniel 9 that an idol will be set up on the wing or pinnacle of the temple, and the apostle John tells of the making of an image of the Roman (Revelation 13:14, 15). Worship will apparently be demanded for the idol and for the ruler it represents.

The second half (three and one-half years) of the seventieth week is evidently identifiable with the "time, times and half a time" of Daniel 7:25; 12:7; Revelation 12:14; the "forty-two months" of Revelation 11:2; 13:5; and the "thousand two hundred and sixty days" of Revelation 11:3; 12:6. During this period, Israel will suffer the unparalleled horrors of the "great tribulation" until the consummation is reached (c.f., Isaiah 10:23). But the desolator, who causes such trouble, having been used as the instrument of God's anger, will himself be destroyed (c.f. Jeremiah 42:18; 44:6; Isaiah 10:12-15).

 # The Church and Her Hope

THREE YEARS of our Lord's public ministry had expired when, at Caesarea Philippi, He challenged His disciples with the question, "Whom say ye that I am?" (Matthew 16:15). He was about to disclose the details of His death, resurrection and Second Advent, but the answer He received from Simon Peter — "Thou art the Christ, the Son of the living God" — evoked another remarkable revelation first. Upon this Rock, i.e., the One whom Peter had confessed (for the term "Rock" is used figuratively in Scripture only of God and never of man), our Lord declared He would build His church. Obviously, at that date and in the sense in which He used the word, the church was still future. It is true that the word *ecclesia*, which Christ employed, means simply an assembly of people and that it has this non-theological meaning in more than one New Testament passage. In Acts 7:38, for example, Israel is described as an assembly (*ecclesia*) or gathering of people in the wilderness; in Acts 19:39 the town clerk of Ephesus referred to the regular assembly (*ecclesia*) of citizens, and in verse 41 he is stated to have dismissed the assembly (same word) or gathering of people who had come together excitedly and without premeditation (see verse 32); in Hebrews 2:12 the writer, quoting Psalm 22:22, uses the same word in relation to a gathering of people for a religious service. But at

Caesarea Philippi our Lord imparted to the word, in addition, a technical significance which it has since consistently retained. Except where they are clearly referring to ordinary gatherings of people, the New Testament writers use the word to cover all Christians (Acts 12:1; I Corinthians 15:9) and also to describe local companies of Christians (Acts 8:1; 9:31; 11:22).

The apostle stated in the epistle to the Ephesians that the church (which he described in Ephesians 1:22, 23 as the body of Christ) was a mystery, hidden in previous ages but revealed in the present age by the Holy Spirit. No direct reference was made to it in the Old Testament, and there was no prophecy regarding it. Until the death of Christ, the purposes of God seemed to be centered in Israel, but in this era Gentiles are fellow-heirs with Jews and members of the same body (Ephesians 3:6), and all national and racial differences are ignored in the divine economy. Jew and Gentile are baptized by the Spirit into the body of Christ (I Corinthians 12:13), and that "body" is not merely a company of believers but a living organism, indwelt by Christ as the hope of glory (Colossians 1:26, 27). "By His coming at the day of Pentecost upon that company of men and women in the upper room," says Dr. Campbell Morgan, "the Holy Ghost formed the Church of Jesus Christ. There had been no church prior to that coming of the Spirit. Individual Jewish disciples had gathered around the Lord during the days of His ministry, and He prepared them for the ushering in of this dispensation. As they gathered together day by day in the upper room, they were a collection of separate, individual souls; but 'when the day of Pentecost was fully come,' and the Spirit fell upon them, He united them into one whole body, the Church of Jesus Christ. The Spirit came to create the church, to be the bond of its life; and from that time to this, men have only entered the church through the new creation of the Spirit." In previous dispensations, the Holy Spirit came upon individuals to equip them for special tasks (Exodus 31:3; Ezekiel 2:2), to use them for the delivery of God's messages (II Chronicles 20:14), to impart a special revelation (Ezekiel 11:1), etc. He came upon them on specific occasions (Numbers 11:25; Judges 14:6) and withdrew when the work was done or the need ended. But in this age, the Holy Spirit indwells the believer personally (I Corinthians 3:16; 6:19) and also the church collectively (Ephesians 2:22).

The present dispensation commenced at Pentecost, as the apostle Peter implied when he related how the Holy Ghost fell on the Gentiles "as on us *at the beginning*" (Acts 11:15). During this era, God's relationship is with the church and not with any other elect body. Prior to the Cross, our Lord's ministry in general excluded the Gentile and was specifically directed to the Jew (e.g., Matthew 10:5, 6), but His purpose now is largely to "visit the Gentiles, to take out of them a people for His name" (Acts 15:14). As the apostle Paul stated very clearly in his epistle to the Romans, "blindness in part is happened to Israel, until the fullness of the Gentiles be come in" (Romans 11:25). Until the outcalling of the church has been completed, Israel is ignored in the divine program. Prior to Pentecost, Israel was God's "elect" (Isaiah 45:4), but during the present day, His elect are the members of His church (I Peter 2:9; Romans 8:33; Colossians 3:12), although in a future day Israel is again to be the chosen and blessed of God (Romans 11:26-28; Isaiah 61:6; 62:4). Israel's future blessing obviously cannot occur until the present parenthesis in Divine dealings with the nation comes to an end with the removal of the elect of today. It was the expectation of early believers that the parenthesis would be relatively brief and that the Lord would speedily return to earth to meet a repentant Israel and to set up His earthly kingdom (e.g., Acts 3:19-21). J. F. Silver demonstrates in *The Lord's Return* that the Apostolic Fathers expected the Lord to return during their lifetime and that the Ante-Nicene Fathers taught the imminent and premillennial return of the Lord.

The duration of the present dispensation is not stated in the Scriptures. It has sometimes been suggested that Revelation 2 and 3 portray the spiritual history of the church; in other words that there must be seven periods of church history corresponding in character to the features described in the letters to the seven churches of Asia. If there is any substance in this view, the fact that there have already been seven such periods is an indication that the age is nearing its end. The similarity between conditions of the last few decades and the description of the last days, given for example in II Timothy 3:1-5, has also convinced many people that the end of this age is not far distant.

The consistent hope of the church has been the return of her Lord. "For our conversation is in heaven; from whence also we look for the Saviour. . . ," wrote the apostle Paul (Philippians 3:20). ". . . ye turned to God from idols to serve the living and true God; and to wait for His Son from heaven. . . ," he reminded the Thessalonians (I Thessalonians 1:9, 10). The exact date of the Lord's coming is not indicated. His statement to Peter made the latter aware that he would die before the coming (John 21:18, 19; II Peter 1:14), but it was generally believed by the disciples that John, on the other hand, would live until the return of his Lord (John 21:23). Peter nevertheless seems to have anticipated the early return of the Saviour (Acts 3:19-21), but Paul knew by revelation that trials and death lay before him (Acts 20:23, 29; 21:11; II Timothy 4:6), while the inspired writers also foretold dissension in the church and apostasy from the truth (Acts 20:29, 30; I Timothy 4:1-3; II Timothy 3:1-5; II Peter 2:1-3; Jude 18). It is clear, therefore, that the Second Advent was not to be expected immediately after our Lord's departure, but that certain events were to be fulfilled before His coming. At the same time, it must have seemed quite conceivable to the early Christians that those events could have happened within a very short space of time and that no serious delay needed then to have been envisaged. As Professor H. C. Thiessen pertinently remarks in *Will the Church Pass Through the Tribulation?* the early church fathers, "held not only the premillennial view of Christ's coming, but also regarded that coming as imminent. The Lord had taught them to expect His return at any moment, and so they looked for Him to come in their day . . . The early church lived in the constant expectation of their Lord." They knew not when He would come and were enjoined to vigilance because they knew not the hour of His return, but this only encouraged them, as Calvin, says, "to be prepared to expect Him every day, or rather every hour."

It is clear from Biblical prophecy that our Lord's return to earth as King will be preceded by a period of unparalleled judgment, during which the wrath of God will be poured out upon the guilty (Revelation 6 to 16). So awful will be this time that the Master referred to it as one of "great tribulation such as was not since the beginning of the world" (Matthew 24:21). It is frequently maintained that the Christian cannot expect his Lord's return until the earth has suffered this period; in other words, that at least some Christians must pass through the Great Tribulation. It is evident, however, that this period is one of wrath and judgment upon the unbeliever (Romans 1:18; Ephesians 2:3; 5:6; II Thessalonians 1:8) and is irrelevant to the church. While the church is to experience tribulation in this world (John 15: 20; Romans 5:3), the believer of this age has been delivered from the oncoming wrath and has not been appointed thereto (I Thessalonians 1:10; 5:9; Romans 5:9). So far as the world is concerned the outbreak of wrath ("the day of the Lord," to which so many of the Old Testament prophets refer as the time of judgment) will come "as a thief in the night," but Christians are "all the children of light and the children of the day;" consequently it will not come upon them as a thief (I Thessalonians 5:2-5). The wrath of God abides upon the unbeliever (John 3:36) and, by inference, the believer is safe therefrom. As one writer says, "it is inconceivable that the church will suffer the wrath of God. The Word of God is very clear in its teaching that those who have found salvation through the shed blood of Christ are thereby forever delivered from the wrath of God, which is revealed from heaven against all ungodliness and unrighteousness of men" (Romans 1:18).

In Revelation 3:10 our Lord specifically promised to keep the Philippian believers "from the hour of temptation, which shall come upon all the world, to try them that dwell upon the earth." Professor Thiessen says that "the word 'dwell' used here (*katoikes*) is a strong word. It is used to describe the fullness of the Godhead that dwelt in Christ (Colossians 2:9); it is used of Christ's taking up a permanant abode in the believer's heart (Ephesians 3:17); and of demons returning to take absolute possession of a man (Matthew 12:45; Luke 11:26). It is to be distinguished from the word *oikeo*, which is the general term for 'dwell,' and *paroikeo*, which has the idea of transitoriness, 'to sojourn.' Thayer remarks that the term *katoikeo* has the idea of permanence in it. Thus the judgment referred to in Revelation 3:10 is directed against earth-dwellers of that day, against those who have settled down in the earth as their real home, who have identified themselves with earth's commerce and religion." This description is quite inappropriate to the Christian, whose citizenship and calling are heavenly and not earthly.

A more novel theory is that the church will be raptured after the first half of Daniel's seventieth "week" (Daniel 9:27). This mid-tribulation theory teaches that the church must go through the "beginning of sorrows" (Matthew 24:8), but not through the dark hours of the Great Tribulation. This is even less logical than the theory already referred to since it necessitates an overlap in the Divine programs for the Church and Israel. In *Kept from the Hour*, Prof. G. B.

Stanton demonstrates conclusively that there is no Scriptural support for the "tribulation theory" or any of its variants (mid-tribulation or post-tribulation rapture), but that the future of the church and all her expectations are heavenly and not earthly in character. The great tribulation is of particular relevance to Israel and is designed to prepare the nation for the coming of the Messiah (Jeremiah 30:7; Ezekiel 20:37; Daniel 12:1; Zechariah 13:8, 9).

The Lord's coming is presented to the church as a blessed hope (Titus 2:13; James 5:7, 8), as a basis of comfort (I Thessalonians 4:18; 5:11; II Thessalonians 2:17;), and as an imminent event (James 5:8; Revelation 22:20; Hebrews 10:37). These descriptions would be quite inaccurate if the prospect of the church was a period of unparalleled suffering and judgment.

Before the day of the Lord comes, II Thessalonians 2:3 declares that there must first be "a falling away", the words used being *hee apostasia, "the apostasy."* This expression normally means defection, revolt or rebellion, but it can also be translated by disappearance or departure, and it has been suggested by K. S. Wuest in *Prophetic Light in the Present Darkness* and by E. S. English in *Rethinking the Rapture,* that the reference is not to an apostasy from the faith, but to a translation of the church from this world. Wuest points out that the word *apostasia* is derived from the root verb *aphisteemi,* which means to remove, withdraw, depart, go away, etc. Of its fifteen occurrences in the New Testament, it is eleven times translated "depart", and he accordingly argues that the substantive must mean "departure" and, since the Greek text has the definite article, a particular departure, i.e., the removal of the church. Whether this is accepted or not, it is obvious that the presence on earth of the church — "the salt of the earth" (Matthew 5:13) — is an obstacle to the spread of corruption and that the full outbreak of sin is held in check so long as the church is here. II Thessalonians 2:6, 7 indicates that the manifestation of the Man of Sin is not possible until the restraining influence has been withdrawn. It has been variously argued that the "restrainer" referred to was the Roman empire, the Jewish State, the devil, Gentile dominion, and the church, but it is evident that the restraining power is the Holy Spirit. No other is capable of holding evil in check to such an extent; indeed, it is one of His functions to strive against sin (Genesis 6:3). The Holy Spirit and the church which He indwells must, therefore, be removed before the Man of Sin appears (presumably at the commencement of the seventieth heptad of Daniel 9).

The day of the Lord, (i.e. the period of God's wrath) will end with the return of Christ to the earth in power and glory (Zechariah 14:1-5; Matthew 24:29, 30). Our Lord promised to take His followers to heaven when He came forth (John 14:3), but when He issues forth in power, His redeemed people will be with Him (I Thessalonians 3:13; Revelation 19:14). Plainly, therefore, they must previously have been taken away. In I Thessalonians 4:14-17 the apostle Paul provides the explanation: the Lord will descend to the air; the dead in Christ will be raised; then all living believers will be caught up with them to meet the Lord in the air and to be for ever with Him. In I Corinthians 15:51, 52 he further reveals that not all believers will die, but that all (alive or dead) will be transformed instantaneously at this coming of the Lord. These facts were a mystery not revealed in the Old Testament, but disclosed only through the medium of the apostle. The church age, which began at Pentecost, will therefore conclude with the sudden translation of all who belong to Christ, and this will happen before God's resumption of His relationship with Israel and before the unfulfilled prophecies of the Old Testament come to fruition. It is often taught that the Old Testament patriarchs will be raised at the same time as the Christians who have died, but the phrase "the dead in Christ" obviously precludes this. The expression "in Christ" is consistently used in the New Testament regarding those who have been baptized by the Holy Spirit into the body of Christ. It is never used of Old Testament saints, and their resurrection will not take place until the end of the great tribulation (Daniel 12:1, 2).

It is sometimes urged that the "trumpet" of I Thessalonians 4:16 and I Corinthians 15:52 is identical with the seventh trumpet of Revelation 11:15, but the Apocalyptic trumpets are of wrath, whereas that of which Paul speaks is one of blessing. Nor can it be identical with the trumpet of Matthew 24:31 which relates to the regathering of Israel (Isaiah 27:12, 13). The term used by the apostle was a military one and in harmony with the other military terms used in the context (e.g. the *order* or *brigade* of I Corinthians 15:23, and the military *shout* of command of I Thessalonians 4:16). When an army was about to move, the soldiers struck their tents and packed their baggage at the sound of the trumpet; when the second trumpet sounded, they fastened their kits to their mules; and at the last trumpet they moved away. The expressions used by the apostle were both significant and appropriate.

It has been stated by a number of writers that the idea of a pretribulation rapture of the church originated in January, 1832, when a certain Emily Cardale (one writer suggests instead that it was Margaret McDonald) gave utterance to it in the Rev. Edward Irving's church in London (see Dr. S. P. Tregelles' *The Hope of Christ's Second Coming*), but it is probable that the Rev. Tweedy had propounded it earlier. William Kelly in *The Rapture of the Saints*, in fact, states that J. N. Darby had adopted it in 1830, but it seems clear that the Christians at Thessalonica were taught the same doctrine by the apostle Paul nearly eighteen centuries earlier. A study of the progress of dogma reveals as suggested in Chapter I that attention was focused first on apologetics, then on theology, anthropology and later on Christology, these being followed by soteriology and ecclesiology, and that only during the last century or so was much notice given to eschatology. Consequently, although the writings of the early Fathers show that the belief in our Lord's early and pre-millennial return was firmly held, they do not discuss to any extent the details of the prophetic program, and it was not until the nineteenth century that Biblical study and understanding brought the detailed truth to light.

Just over a century ago, in *Entrance into the Kingdom*, Robert Govett propounded the theory that the future blessing of Christians was not unconditional, but was dependent upon their vigilance and fidelity. According to this teaching, not all believers will be caught up to meet the Lord when He comes, but only those who are actually watching for Him; only these will hear His voice and, therefore, share in the first resurrection (John 5:25). Others, Govett and his followers concluded, will be left behind to be punished in the fires of suffering of the great tribulation. G. H. Pember writes, "Those who are translated will have to be accounted worthy of it; it is not a gift, but a prize to be won, in the strength of the Lord, by the fruits of faith, conduct and works after conversion." But the New Testament makes it clear that rewards for service are to be bestowed at the judgment seat of Christ, and that while they may be described, for example, as a crown of life or of glory, they are not to be confused with the rapture itself. (I Corinthians 9:25; II Corinthians 5:10; II Timothy 4:8; James 1:12; I Peter 5:4; Revelation 2:10).

The relationship of the believer to Christ is based from beginning to end on grace, but the selective rapture theory insists upon works as the ground for the believer's rapture to meet his Lord. "All the passages dealing . . . with the requisites for rapture," says D. M. Panton, "assert personal watchfulness and worthiness as essential; the *ready* virgin alone enters (Matthew 25:10); the *ready* householder alone is unrobbed (Matthew 24:44); the *ready* disciple alone is rapt (Luke 17:34) — 'therefore, be ye also ready'. . . . It is the natural inference from our Lord's words that it is the unwatchfulness of the one left, and his unwatchfulness only, that has prevented his rapture." An examination of the Scriptures quoted, however, reveals that they relate, not to the coming of Christ for the church, but to the return of the Son of Man in judgment. Moreover, there are not lacking Scriptures which plainly show that the translation of the Christian is *not* dependent upon his watchfulness (e.g., I Thessalonians 1:9, 10; 2:19; 5:4-11; Revelation 22:12). The apostle's statement is perfectly clear that, whether we watch or sleep, we shall live with Christ (I Thessalonians 5:10). It is not dependent upon our vigilance but upon His grace.

By the work of Christ, as Pentecost points out in *Things to Come,* the sinner is justified, made acceptable to God, placed in Christ positionally to be received by God as though he were the Son Himself. The individual who has this perfect standing of Christ can never be less than completely acceptable to God. The partial rapture theory minimizes the fact of this standing of the believer and insists upon personal experiential righteousness as his qualification to be caught up to meet the Lord.

Many of the Scriptures quoted by the protagonists of this theory are not strictly relevant. For example, it is assumed that Luke 21:36 applies to unwatchful Christians, whereas it clearly relates to the period of the great tribulation, and what is to be escaped is the judgment associated with the day of the Lord. The references in Matthew 24 to one being taken and the other left are found in a discourse outlining Israel's future experiences, and they do not concern the church or the Christian. Philippians 3:10-12 is often cited as proving that all Christians will not be included in the first resurrection, but this passage refers to spiritual aspirations in the present life and not to the attainment of the first resurrection. The phrase "every man

in his own order" (I Corinthians 15:23) in connection with
the resurrection, is sometimes claimed to be evidence that
members of the church will be raised at different periods
according to the degree of their fidelity to Christ, but it is
clear that the words refer to resurrection as a whole and
not merely to the church. There is no indication that the
church will not be removed as a complete entity. Believers
of the present day are members of the body of Christ (I
Corinthians 12:12, 13; Ephesians 5:30), and, as Prof. Walvoord pertinently remarks, "the Scriptures teach that the
body of Christ, composed of all true believers, is a unit and
is given promises as such."

No dismembered or defective body, but a complete one,
will be taken when the Lord comes. Our position before
God is not dependent upon our own merit or morality, our
vigilance or fidelity; it is dependent upon the work of
Christ, and our hope of translation is based, not upon
our endeavours, but upon His promises.

Passages such as Titus 2:13 and Hebrews 9:28 are sometimes quoted as supporting the idea of a selective rapture,
but these Scriptures merely indicate the proper attitude
of expectation which should be that of every believer; they
do not imply that looking or waiting is a condition of translation. It would be profitless to examine all the texts which
are used as arguments in support of the theory; many are
not really pertinent and none appear to furnish any sub-
stantial basis for the acceptance of the idea.

In *Prophecy and the Church*, Dr. Oswald T. Allis draws
attention to the disturbing fact that, "the doctrine of a partial rapture practically necessitates the acceptance of the
Romish doctrine of purgatory. For it must be admitted
that many Christians have died, to all appearances in the
imperfect state which, we are told, will characterize those
who at the rapture are left on earth to be purified by the
great tribulation. So, unless it is held that, in the very
article of death, they have or will have endured purifying

or chastening sufferings equivalent to those which will be endured by those who are left behind at the time of the rapture, the argument that these latter need to pass through the tribulation falls to the ground, unless the doctrine of purgatory is accepted. The dying thief was, in all probability, a very imperfect and a very ignorant believer. But the Lord said to him, 'Today thou shalt be with Me in paradise.' " The church is inseparably connected with her Head, and when He returns, every member of the church, whether alive or dead, will be caught up to meet Him in the air. It is for this we hope and wait, and we believe that it will not long be delayed.

The rapture of the church must be followed by the examination of the life and work of the Christian at the judgment seat of Christ (see Chapter VI) as a necessary preliminary to the marvellous event described by the Revelation as "the marriage of the Lamb." Walvoord says, a "Hebrew marriage has three stages: (1) the legal marriage consummated by the parents of the bride and groom; (2) the groom goes to take His bride from her parents' home; (3) the wedding supper or feast. Most Greek scholars take the Greek word *gamos*, translated 'marriage' in Revelation 19:7 to mean 'wedding feast'." The espousal has already taken place (II Corinthians 11:2; Romans 7:4) and the Bridegroom will shortly come for His bride. The marriage feast took place in the home of the groom and his parents. Appropriately, therefore, our Lord declared that He was going to prepare a place in His Father's house and would then come for His bride (John 14:2, 3). At the marriage feast, the bride will be clad in "the righteousness of the saints." The actions which glorified her Lord during her earthly path will be her robe on the day of nuptial bliss.

The union is, of course, a public testimony to the inhabitants of the celestial heights of Christ's love for His church and His intention to share His glory and His possessions with her. When He issues forth in power and glory, His beloved will be with Him. In a day to come, Christ will be supreme throughout the whole vast creation of God, and the church is to share His glory with Him.

CHAPTER VI

The Judgment Seat of Christ

WRITING TO believers at Corinth, the apostle Paul said, "we must all be manifested before the judgment seat of Christ; that every one may receive the things done in his body, according to that he hath done, whether it be good or bad" (II Corinthians 5:10). This cannot, of course, refer to any condemnatory judgment. Our Lord specifically stated that the one who believes God "shall not come into judgment" (John 5:24), and the apostle declared that there is no condemnation for those who are in Christ Jesus (Romans 8:1). As A. Pridham says, "A saint will never again come into judgment on account of his natural or inherited iniquity, for he is already dead judicially with Christ, and is no longer known or dealt with on the footing of his natural responsibility. . . . He is justified by faith. . . . Into judgment, therefore, on his own account, he cannot come." The judgment seat of Christ cannot, therefore, be identical with the final assize at the great white throne, for there the spiritually "dead" are to be judged and condemned and the penal sentence passed upon them will be immediately executed (Revelation 20:11-15). But the judgment seat of Christ is concerned with believers (this is made clear, *inter alia*, by the pronoun used consistently throughout II Corinthians 5), and there can be no question of penal judgment for them.

Nor has this judgment seat any relation to purgatorial suffering. It has been argued that unconfessed sin must necessarily be a barrier to entry into eternal bliss and that one with unconfessed sin on his conscience must consequently suffer for his wrongdoing before entering into blessing. This theory is without Scriptural support. It is beyond the ability of man to atone for his own sin, and the future blessing of the saved sinner is dependent, not upon him, but upon his Lord. The "suffering" of I Corinthians 3:15 has, of course, no other significance than the losing of a reward which others have gained.

Plummer says that the *bema* (the word translated "judgment seat") was "the tribunal, whether in a basilica for the praetor in a court of justice, or in a camp for the commander to administer discipline and address the troops." On the Areopagus at Athens, it was a stone platform. At the Olympic Games in ancient Greece, the arena contained a raised stone or wooden platform, i.e., *a bema,* on which the judge would sit and award the prizes to the victorious competitors. Paul takes up the same figure and the same word and applies them to the Christian and his Lord. A greater Judge is one day to sit on another *bema* to examine the lives and service of His followers and to bestow rewards for faithfulness and to leave the careless, self-centered and unfaithful to suffer loss. The antinomian heresy, which suggests that life does not matter because salvation is secure, is both unscriptural and ill-considered. We are to give an account of ourselves to God.

The assessment of life cannot finally take place until we are removed from this scene, but it is clear from Revelation 19:7, 8 that it will precede the marriage of the Lamb, since reference is made to the righteousness of the saints, which will have clearly survived the examination at the *bema.* The judgment seat must, therefore, follow the rapture of the church and precede her marriage to her Lord.

If life is to be reviewed and its value assessed by the

righteous Judge, it would seem necessary either for the events of the past to be recalled or else for an authoritative record of them to be produced. The presumption of such a necessity is naturally based upon the human conception of time as past, present and future, but this is not a completely reliable view. The astronomer may gaze through his telescope at stars from which the light he sees has been travelling two thousand years or two million years; he sees them both today, although what he sees relates to varying times in the past. Time is only relative. In *The Transitoriness of Life*, F. W. Robertson writes, "With God there is no time — it is one eternal NOW. . . . There are spots in the universe which have not yet been reached by the beams of light which shone from this earth at its creation. If, therefore, we were able on an angel's wings to reach that spot in a second or two of time, the sight of this globe would be just becoming visible as it was when chaos passed into beauty. A few myriad miles nearer, we should be met by the picture of the world in the state of deluge. And so, in turn, would present themselves the spectacles of patriarchal life; of Assyrian, Grecian, Persian, Roman civilizations; and, at a short distance from the earth, the scenes of yesterday. Thus a mere transposition in space would make the past present. And thus, all that we need is the annihilation of space to annihilate time. So that, if we conceive a Being present everywhere in space, to Him all past events would be present. At the remotest extremity of the angel's journey, he would see the world's creation. At this extremity, the events that pass before our eyes today. Omnipresence in space is thus equivalent to ubiquity in time. And to such a Being demonstrably there would be no time. All would be one vast eternal NOW." The recall of events which have happened in what we term "the past," therefore, presents no problem to the Almighty.

The physicist can demonstrate that matter is indestructible, but it seems clear that the immaterial has a permanent existence as well as the material and that everything that has happened in this world continues to be. For example, words uttered centuries ago set sound waves rippling through space. Although the sound has apparently died away, the waves remain, and it may yet be possible to detect and record the sound.

The full record of the individual's life and actions is held in his own memory. Everything he has said and done has left an impression on his mind. Some things seem to have been obliterated from memory, but the initial impression was ineradicable, and a touch of a Divine finger to deepen that impression or to make memory more acute would cause the whole of the past to flood back into active thought once more.

Moreover, our lives impinge upon those of other people, and what we do and say has its effect upon those with whom we come into contact, and *vice versa*. A benevolent act will never fade from the recollection of the beneficiary, while an unkind remark may leave an unforgettable wound. Not only from our own memories, but also from the memories of others might be culled details of much of our lives. But, by whatever means it may be, life will be revealed in detail at the heavenly *bema*. ". . . we shall all stand before the judgment seat of Christ . . . So then every one of us shall give account of himself to God" (Romans 14:10-12).

The question is often asked whether the examination of the Christian's life at the *bema* will be conducted publicly or privately. There is no indication regarding this in the New Testament, but it seems reasonable to assume that the Master's tender compassion will mercifully hide any personal shame of His people from the eyes of others so far as is fair and practicable. Yet it cannot be ignored that others may be implicated as the story of life is re-told. In some cases wrongs committed on earth have never been rectified; in others reconciliations which should have been effected during our human life have never been made. In such instances the simultaneous presence at the *bema* of both parties concerned — the wronged one and the one who committed the wrong — seems essential if matters are to be righted and justice to be done. There is no reason to suppose, however, that personal failures and weaknesses will be exposed generally to the critical gaze of others.

The assessment of life's value will take into consideration all the relevant factors and not merely the positive actions taken before the eyes of all. Indeed, in the Sermon on the Mount (Matthew 5), our Lord made it clear that He was more interested in motives than in overt actions. As a man thinketh in his heart, so is he. What a man does may be in no respect a true revelation of his character; worthy deeds may be prompted by unworthy motives, and noble words may be inspired by base intentions. Superficial values are not always identical with true values. The Lord Jesus Christ is the searcher of the thoughts and intents of the heart. He discerns the reason for the actions we take and the motives which prompt the doing, and His assessment of the value of a particular action will be based on the character of the desire that motivated it. Insincerity and unreality are open to Him, and honesty and truth are plain to His omniscient eye. He is cognizant both of the initial impulse and of the end it was hoped to achieve. We inevitably judge on externals, but His assessment is related to the inner movements of the heart and mind. In consequence, there is no duplication of rewards nor any loss of what is morally due. One whose object was to secure some mundane end will receive no additional reward on Christ's estimation. On the other hand, one whose performance was imperfect but whose heart was true will not lose his reward simply because his work seemed small.

It is apparent from our Lord's teaching that a fair assessment of the value of a man's work must of necessity take account of the natural and spiritual endowments originally bestowed upon him by God. In the parable of the talents

(Matthew 25:14-30), the Master revealed that varying abilities are given to individuals and that the estimate of a servant's work pays regard to this fact. In the parable, the noble gave to one of his servants five talents, to another two talents, and to a third only one talent. The first, by trading, gained five more talents; the second, by his industry, acquired two more; while the third merely buried his talent. On their master's return, the servants were summoned to give account of their stewardship. The first two were commended by their master for their faithfulness, and it is significant that the commendation and the promised reward of the second were identical with those of the first. It is true that the actual amount produced by his labours was only forty per cent of the amount produced by the first, but it was exactly one hundred per cent return on the amount originally entrusted to him. As this was true also of the first, the measure of faithfulness shown was equivalent, and the rewards were, therefore, equivalent too. By implication, Christ will take account of the gifts bestowed upon His servants and will estimate the value of the work they do by its relation to the endowments originally bestowed. From the one to whom much has been given, much will be expected; from the one to whom little has been given, correspondingly less will be expected. The more gifted the individual, the greater his responsibility to his Master.

In the somewhat similar parable of the pounds (Luke 19:11-26), our Lord made it clear that equal opportunities of service (even if in different spheres) are afforded to all and that He will pay regard to the differing degrees of diligence shown. To each of his servants, the nobleman of this parable entrusted the same amount of money — one pound — directing each of them to trade with it until he returned. When the accounting day eventually arrived, one servant reported that he had acquired ten more pounds by the use of his pound, while another stated that he had gained five. In commending the first for his diligence, the nobleman also bestowed a reward upon him which was directly related to the measure of his industry — he was set in authority over ten cities. The commendation of the second servant also included a reward; he had gained five pounds and was appointed over five cities. The basis of the rewards was perfectly fair and equitable. Our Lord thus made it plain that He will not only take into account the gifts and varying abilities possessed by His servants, but also the diligence and industry demonstrated in the use of what is held. It would be unfair to expect equality of return by servants whose gifts (and consequent potentialities) are so varied. It would be equally unjust if, after making allowance for the personal ability or inability, no account was taken of faithful service. The theory that all will be equally blessed in a future day, irrespective of the manner in which they have lived, is without Scriptural foundation.

It matters how we live, since what is done on earth will have its effect in eternity. Just as the servant who buried his one talent in the earth and the one who wrapped up his one talent in a napkin suffered permanent loss, so will the slothful and indolent Christian not only experience the loss of reward at the *bema*, but also be deprived for eternity of what he might have attained. ". . . hold that fast which thou hast, that no man take thy crown," said the risen Lord (Revelation 3:11). What we are now determines what we shall be for all eternity. The bride of the Lamb's marriage is to be clothed in the righteous works of the saints (Revelation 19:8).

Lest it should be concluded that future rewards will be determined principally by the actual quantum or the superficial value of the results produced, our Lord set matters in their right perspective by declaring that the giving of a cup of cold water *in His name* would attract a reward (Mark 9:41). In other words, the determining factor will not be any human estimate of values but the extent of the love and devotion to Him. He places more weight upon the deeds of a loving heart than upon the marvellous exploits of a self-centered spirit. The ostentatious and the spectacular receive the applause of men, but the Master's eye detects what we would term trivialities, and it is possible that our sense of values is completely inaccurate.

Using remarkable imagery, the apostle Paul describes the believer's life as a city over which will have passed the scorching flames of a great fire in all their destructive force (I Corinthians 3:11-15), and implies that future rewards will be determined by the extent to which the life is capable of standing the test of the fire. Right through the valley in which the city was built ran a solid rock foundation on which every building was founded. The buildings themselves were of the utmost variety. The great majority, occupied by the artisans and the slaves, were simple cottages constructed of wood and thatched with hay or straw. In close juxtaposition stood the impressive mansions of the wealthy and noble. From the center of the city rose a magnificent temple with golden dome, silver filigree and massive pillars, while, in close proximity, stood the ruler's ornate palace with its glistening treasures. Whether it was palace or peasant's hovel, however, every house had been built upon the solid rock, and the apostle, interpreting his own parable, declared that in the spiritual realm the foundation laid is Jesus Christ. Nothing could disturb that solid foundation. Upon Him has been built every redeemed soul, and upon Him every one continues to build with his own materials.

Suddenly a tongue of fire burst through the roof of one of the cottages and in a matter of minutes the inflammable building was a mass of flames. The fire rapidly spread through the narrow busy streets turning the city into a blazing inferno and consuming every combustible object within reach. It swept round the temple and the palace but left them unharmed, but every wooden cottage was reduced to ashes. As presently the flames died down, men were seen turning over the debris and the smoking ruins, only to discover that all their belongings had perished in the fire. The gold, silver and precious stones had stood the test, but the wood, hay and stubble had completely disappeared.

"Every man's work shall be made manifest," wrote the apostle, "for the day shall declare it, because it shall be revealed by fire; and the fire shall try every man's work of what sort it is. If any man's work abide . . . he shall receive a reward. If any man's work shall be burned, he shall suffer loss" (I Corinthians 3:12-24). The conflagration provided the apostle with a vivid illustration of the future day of testing at the *bema*, when life will be scrupulously examined and every man's work will be brought under the scorching fire of Divine holiness. The material of which life has been constructed will then be brought to the test; the combustible wood, hay and stubble will be destroyed, and only the gold, silver and precious stones will abide the fire. Wood, the lifeless timber so aptly figurative of dead works, will be destroyed. Hay, the worthless, inconsequential and insubstantial character of the superficial life, will perish in the flames. Stubble, the remnants of a former glory, will be reduced to ashes. But the gold, so symbolic of the work inspired by God and undertaken for His glory, will stand the test. Silver, the reminder of the Old Testament price of redemption and the suggestion of the works of a redeemed life, will be unharmed by the flames. Precious stones, in all their radiant beauty reflecting and refracting the glorious colours of the light like the life reflecting the glories of Christ, will be untouched by the fire.

The examination at the judgment seat will determine what is acceptable and what is worthless. (The word *phaulos*, translated "bad" in II Corinthians 5:10, does not imply what is ethically or morally evil, but rather what is worthless). It is a salutary thought that, after all his life of service for Christ, the apostle Paul should still be concerned lest eventually he might be disapproved (I Corinthians 9:27).

The *bema* will not only be the scene of examination but also of reward. There is a prize to be won (I Corinthians 9:24, 25), and the apostle Paul patently anticipated receiving the reward of his service and loyalty to Christ. "And behold, I come quickly;" said our Lord, "and My reward is with me, to give to every man according as his work shall be" (Revelation 22:12). That the service rendered by the Christian should be deserving of notice at all seems incredible; yet the Master is pleased to take account of everything that is done in his name, and in that day He will assess the value of what has been done and bestow His reward on this basis of His valuation. "In the New Testament," says Dr. J. D. Pentecost, "there are five areas in which specific mention is made of a reward: (1) an incorruptible crown for those who get the mastery over the old man (I Corinthians 9:25); (2) a crown of rejoicing for the soulwinners (I Thessalonians 2:19); (3) a crown of life for those enduring trials (James 1:12); (4) a crown of righteousness for loving His appearing (II Timothy 4:8); and (5) a crown of glory for being willing to feed the flock of God (I Peter 5:4)." There is an implication in the parable of the pounds (Luke 19:12-26) that the rewards bestowed upon Christians may take the form of territorial authority. The whole of creation is the possession of Christ, and it is not fanciful to assume that the administration of some of the celestial spheres may be delegated by our Lord to His people.

 # The Gentile Kingdoms

1. THE WESTERN POWER

Two and one-half millennia ago, Nebuchadnezzar lay on his couch, evidently cogitating on the future of the great emipre in the building of which he had played such a significant part. Powerful and independent, he had fought his way upward by his own unaided efforts. As he lay thinking of hs achievements and of the glories of the Babylon he had built, his thoughts turned to the tormenting question: what would happen after this? His own span of life was naturally limited. What would happen after him? Would the empire he had created continue to develop in might and power, or would it crumple up when his strong hand and dominant personality had been withdrawn? His secret thoughts were suddenly and unexpectedly answered, and the future world sovereignty was divinely revealed to him (Daniel 2:31-45).

The king saw in a dream a gigantic human image constructed principally of metal, the head being of gold, the breast and arms of silver, the abdomen and hips of copper (or bronze), the thighs of iron, and the feet of iron mingled with clay. A stone, quarried without human agency, fell upon the feet of the image, breaking them to pieces and bringing the whole structure toppling to the ground to smash to powder. The pulverized fragments of the colossus were dispersed by the wind, and not a trace was left of the immense image. The stone then rapidly expanded into a great mountain, so tremendous in size that it filled the whole earth.

There was no doubt as to the meaning of the dream, for an inspired interpretation was given to the king through the prophet Daniel. The latter declared plainly that God had seen fit to disclose to the monarch the future, not only of his own empire, but of those which should follow Babylon. The Almighty Sovereign of the skies, in whose hands all the threads of power are ultimately gathered up and held, had invested Nebuchadnezzar with universal dominion. That he did not exercise all the rights and privileges entrusted to him, or that he did not extend the borders of his kingdom to the extreme limit, was immaterial; potentially the world was his; he was "a king of kings". He was the golden head portrayed in the image (Daniel 2:38).

The prophecy made it clear, however, that the Chaldean empire with all its glory and wealth would eventually be superseded by another power, of which the silver breast and arms were an apt symbol. As Daniel 5:28-31 confirms, this actually took place. Babylon was subdued, and the kingdom was absorbed by the Medo-Persians. This second empire in turn gave place to the Macedonian empire founded by Alexander the Great (Daniel 8:21), the extent of whose authority, as the prophecy foretold, was almost universal. The third empire was superseded in due course by a fourth, not specifically named in the Book of Daniel, but there is no question regarding its identity, for Luke 2:1 makes it plain that at that time Rome had succeeded to world sovereignty. It is usually claimed that the deterioration in the quality of the metallic constituents of the image (gold, silver, copper, iron) is reflected in the character of the rule of the different empires, and there is some justification for this view.

When the four world-empires had run their course, the prophecy foretold that the kingdoms would be crushed, and God would establish the kingdom of the heavens on earth. Although the four great powers seen in symbol by Nebuchadnezzar have long since passed away, the long-promised theocratic kingdom has never appeared. In this respect the prophecy has never been fulfilled. Other empires have made their appearance on the scene, but none of them is referred to in the prophetic word.

In the first year of Belshazzar, when the glory of Babylon had begun to wane, a further revelation was given to Daniel through the medium of a dream (Daniel 7:1-14). The prophet's dream provided a complete confirmation of Nebuchadnezzar's vision of the course of imperial rule. But whereas the heathen monarch saw a composite image, the prophet saw the individual powers separately and in their true character arising out of the sea. The sea is, of course, frequently used in Scripture as a type of the restless nations (Isaiah 17:12; Revelation 17:15) and is appropriately used in the context of the vision. In Daniel's dream, the Chaldean empire appeared as a lion with eagle's wings, the Medo-Persian as a bear raised on one side, the Grecian as a winged leopard with four heads, and the Roman as a terrible nondescript beast. Secular history shows how remarkably pertinent the descriptions were, and it is not surprising that some of the critics should have been misled into assuming that the Biblical account was written after and not before the events described. (Readers who are interested will find a fuller examination of the details in the author's book, *The Climax of the Ages*). Following the destruction of the last beast, the prophet saw in the vision the glorious installation of Christ as the supreme Ruler over the earth. Once again, no reference of any kind is made to the great empires which have played their part in the history of the last fifteen centuries.

In Daniel's dream, as in Nebuchadnezzar's, the events

mentioned appear to follow each other in an unbroken sequence, but the fact remains that, although the four world-empires have had their day and have passed off the scene, the everlasting kingdom which the Ancient of days was to bestow upon the Son of Man has not yet been manifested. Fifteen centuries have elapsed since the destruction of the Roman empire, but the concluding section of the prophecy remains unfulfilled. Some expositors have jumped to the conclusion that the final empire or kingdom of the heavens of Daniel 2 and 7 must, therefore, be regarded as a spiritual one rather than a literal one, and that it has been realized in the present age in the church of God so that no material kingdom is to be expected. It is extremely difficult to reconcile this theory with the plain statements of the prophecies themselves. Nebuchadnezzar's and Daniel's visions were both of four imperial powers, each of which exercised a literal dominion in this world and each of which had a specific geographical location and boundaries. Consistency demands that the fifth empire should be as literal as its predecessors. If, moreover, the kingdom of the heavens is to be identified with the golden age of the prophets — as many expositors consider — it cannot be ignored that many of the particulars given in the Bible of the period of millennial blessing can apply only to an actual earthly kingdom. To spiritualize some of the details would require the utmost ingenuity. On the other hand, a hiatus of fifteen centuries is difficult to explain, except on the basis already mentioned in Chapter IV, viz., that the reckoning of time in prophecy is always linked with the chosen people of Israel. On this assumption, time ceased to count in God's reckoning immediately prior to the death of the Messiah at Calvary, and it will not recommence until the elect people of the present era (i.e., the church) have been removed.

A study of the description given of the fourth empire in Daniel 2 and 7 leads to the conclusion that certain of the details have not been seen in the past history and activities of the Roman empire. Furthermore, there is a clear indication in Daniel 9:27 that a Roman ruler of a day then future would enter into a seven years' treaty with the Jews. At no time since the words were uttered centuries ago has such a treaty been made. We are forced to the conclusion that the history of Rome has not yet finished and that she still has a future part to play upon the world's stage.

This is confirmed by the revelation of the future made in the Apocalypse. Looking on to the latter days after the church has been raptured from the earth, John describes in Revelation 13:1-10 the rise of a beast out of the sea (the same symbol of the restless and troubled nations as is found in Daniel 7). The predominant form of the beast was that of a leopard with feet like those of a bear and a mouth like that of a lion. The characteristics of Daniel's four empires — the lion of Babylon, the bear of Persia, the leopard of Greece, and the iron strength and universal authority of Rome — were all apparent in this later beast. In Daniel's vision, it was disclosed that the fourth empire would be composed of ten kingdoms, out of which would arise a powerful ruler who would subdue three of the federated kingdoms, and then become supreme dictator over the whole empire (Daniel 7:8, 24). Nothing comparable to this has happened in the history of the Roman empire. In the Apocalyptic vision, the beast seen by John had seven heads and ten horns, each of the latter bearing a diadem.

It is evident that John's vision was of the same power as Daniel's, but if so, the obvious conclusion again is that the history of the Roman empire has not yet finished, but that there is (as has already been suggested) still a future for that great power. Indeed, the picture as seen in Daniel 7 is of a condition of the Roman empire which has never yet existed.

The Roman empire has been non-existent for fifteen centuries. When it disintegrated, many petty states and kingdoms sprang into being from the fragments, but they remained separate and unconnected entities. The diademed horns of the beast of Revelation 13:1-8, however, plainly imply that in a future day ten kingdoms will be bound together in one cohesive whole to form a powerful empire of a different character from that of the past. Upon the mighty ruler of the ten kingdoms, the devil will bestow the world-authority which he offered to our Lord on the mountain of temptation (Luke 4:5-8; Revelation 13:2). Daniel's prophecy describes an imperial ruler with "a mouth speaking great things," who wore out the saints of God and whose power lasted for three and one-half years, a period which will apparently synchronize with the three and one-half years of the second half of the period of Daniel's seventieth week (Daniel 9:27). Homage will be paid to him which is obviously more than civil reverence; it will be a religious adoration, since the new Caesar will demand Divine worship as did the deified emperors of earlier days. The description in Daniel finds a parallel in the Revelation where the Apocalyptic beast is described as having "a mouth speaking great things." It is also stated that he will blaspheme God and that he will make war on the saints (i.e., the Jews) and that the authority bestowed upon him will be for a period of forty-two months — evidently the same period of three and one-half years as in Daniel 9:27.

There is a further reference to the same individual in II Thessalonians 2:3-12, where the apostle Paul paints the picture of the future Man of Sin through whose coming idolatry will be introduced. This evil character, according to the apostle, will enter the rebuilt temple at Jerusalem, showing himself as God and claiming that Divine honours shall be paid to him. An additional detail is given in Revelation 13:15, where it is revealed that an idol of the great ruler will be installed in the temple and that life and speech will be miraculously imparted to the idol. One rendering of the middle clause of Daniel 9:27 (A.V. rendering, "for the overspreading of abominations he shall make it desolate") affords an interesting sidelight upon this event: "upon the wing (of the temple) there shall be idols of the desolator." In our Lord's Olivet discourse, there is another hint in His words, "when you see the desolating sacrilege spoken of by the prophet Daniel, standing in the holy place" (R.S.V.).

A second ruler is protrayed by the apostle John as a beast arising out of the earth, i.e., presumably the land of Israel, indicating that he is a Jew. This second beast bore horns like a lamb, but he spoke like a dragon (Revelation 13:11-18). Since the devil is described in the same book as the dragon, it is clear that he is regarded as diabolically inspired. Our Lord will be acknowledged one day as king and priest (Zechariah 6:13), and this apostate Jew seems to be a counterfeit of the true. The apostle refers to him as the false prophet. He is clearly a coadjutor of the first beast and will exercise all his authority before him, although the power delegated to him is to be used primarily for the glorification of his master. It is often suggested that this man is "the willful king" of Daniel 11:36-39, the latter-day governor in Israel. The Apocalypse discloses that he will be possessed of miraculous powers, and it will be he who gives life to the image of the western emperor and enables it to speak. Through his machinations, the worship of the future Caesar will be forced upon both the Jewish and the Gentile subjects of the imperial ruler. By his instrumentality also, absolute control of employers and employees will be secured by forcible registration (described by John as a mark in the right hand or upon the forehead), so that both industry and workpeople will be dependent upon the official will of the central authority (Revelation 13:16, 17).

There seems little doubt that it is the great western emperor who is referred to in Daniel 9:27 — the coming prince who is to enter into a seven years' treaty with Israel (probably headed by the false prophet). The object of the treaty is not stated, but current events show quite clearly

Israel's need for such an alliance as a guarantee of protection against complete annihilation by her hostile neighbours. Halfway through the period of the covenant, the Gentile sovereign will put a stop to Jewish religious practices. Since this will evidently coincide with the setting up of his image in the temple, the object will obviously be the supersession of Jewish worship of God by a universal worship of a man. Our Lord declared that the ensuing period would be one of great tribulation, unparalleled in the world's history, but that it would be brought to an end by His coming in power and great glory (Matthew 24:21-30).

The end of both beasts will come at the return to earth of the Lord Jesus Christ to execute judgment on a guilty world. With all their mighty armies, the western ruler and his subordinate kingdoms will gather to make war on the Son of God but only to be captured and, together with the false prophet, cast for ever into the lake of fire (Revelation 17:13, 14; 19:19-21). No corporeal death will be theirs: their eternal doom is to be consigned for ever to the place of eternal judgment.

2.   THE KINGS OF THE NORTH AND SOUTH

In addition to the western empire other great powers have their part to play upon the prophetic stage, but it is significant that prophecy is concerned only with those powers which impinge in some way upon the nation of Israel.

Twenty years after the death of Alexander the Great, his vast empire was divided between four of his generals. Focusing attention on two of these (Syria and Egypt), Daniel 11 describes the history and the relations between these two kingdoms down to the end-time. In prophecy Palestine is consistently regarded as the center of God's dealings on earth, and all other powers are viewed in relation to it. The two countries of Syria and Egypt are consequently referred to in Daniel as the kings (or kingdoms) of the north and south, since this was actually their geographical position vis-a-vis Palestine.

Daniel 11:5-35 predicts with amazing accuracy the history of the two powers down to the period of Antiochus Epiphanes and the Maccabean struggle, but verse 36 introduces a new character under the term "the king". Many of the characteristics of this man were manifested in Antiochus, but since the king of the north is subsequently said to attack "the king", the latter can scarcely be identified with the Syrian ruler. It seems clear that, as so often in the prophetic word, Daniel leaps over the centuries and refers to events which still lie in the future. The description given of the willful king indicates that he will be a Jew, and there is good reason for identifying him with the apostate who will govern Israel in a coming day — the false prophet of the Apocalypse.

One of the major purposes of the covenant between the western emperor and the Jewish ruler will evidently be to protect the Israeli state from possible invaders, and the apostate nation will boast of its fancied security. "We have made a covenant with death, and with hell are we at agreement; when the overflowing scourge shall pass through, it shall not come unto us: for we have made lies our refuge, and under falsehood have we hid ourselves" (Isaiah 28:15). Despite this, the protection of the western power will be ineffective to prevent the land being attacked. At the end-time Egypt will launch an attack upon Israel (Daniel 11: 40), doubtless in order to settle old scores and to re-establish her prestige. Daniel 11:43 suggests that Egypt will have a far greater influence and authority than in Daniel's day, and that Libya, Ethiopia and Egypt will be allied in a great North African confederacy of very considerable strength. It is clear, however, that Egypt will never be allowed to take over the Middle East and the control of the oil wells and their wealth.

At the southern invasion, the ire of the northern power

will be aroused, and in swift retaliation, he will sweep through the country like a whirlwind. His hosts will cover the land like a cloud, taking possession of half the city of Jerusalem (Zechariah 14:2) and pursuing the Egyptians into Africa. Overflowing into the adjacent countries, the terror-inspiring hosts will leave havoc and devastation behind them. Isaiah's description of the doings of the Assyrian and Joel's of the exploits of the northerner give some impression of the terrors of that period.

With the exception of Edom, Moab and Ammon (i.e., largely the country of Jordan), no country will be able to withstand the terrible weight of the northern onslaught. But the principal foe is evidently Egypt, or the king of the south, and the prophetic word reveals the awful fate that will overtake that ancient land in the day of her trouble. Ezekiel declares that her foundations will be overthrown, the pride of her strength fall, her lands be desolated and her cities be wasted (Ezekiel 30:1-8). The treasures of Egypt will fall into the hands of the northern invader, and the armies of the latter will carry off all the riches of gold, silver and precious stones, denuding the country of everything of value. The text suggests, not just a single act of stripping, but an intention to impose a sustained control of the country and its possessions, so that there would be a constant flow of materials northwards. Egypt is to suffer complete indignity.

At the height of the northern army's victorious invasion of Egypt, disquieting rumours from the north-east (i.e., from Palestine) will reach the mighty conqueror.

When the armies of the north sweep forth to rout the invader of Israel, their first action will be to raise the siege of Jerusalem but also to capture half the city (Zechariah 14:2) before pressing southwards. In the meantime, the Jewish ruler will doubtless have appealed for help to his confederate, the western emperor, in response to which the hosts of the west will pour over Europe to lay siege again to

Jerusalem. In addition, there will be a terrifying invasion from the east. From all directions armed forces will gather in the tiny land of Palestine.

At the crucial moment, a mighty Deliverer will come to Zion to recompense His enemies (Isaiah 31:4-9; 59:18-20), for the Lord will come forth from the heavens to wage war on behalf of His people. At that awful coming, judgment will fall. The western emperor and the Jewish king will be snatched away for condign punishment, and the panic-stricken people will flee. While the northern king is ruthlessly laying Egypt low, rumours of these happenings will reach him and will profoundly disturb him. Infuriated by what he has heard, he will return in mad anger, intent upon quelling the apparent rebellion, exterminating the rebels and rampaging through the land, but he will ignorantly be rushing upon the thick bosses of the Almighty. Back in Palestine, he will plant his royal pavilion with the military tents of his followers in the holy mountain of Zion between the Mediterranean and the Dead Sea and proceed to lay siege to the holy city, little realizing the One with whom he has to do. It is at this stage that Divine retribution falls, and as foretold in Zephaniah 3:8; Joel 3:2, 12, etc., the wrath of God will be poured out upon the gathered armies utterly to consume them. The mighty northerner will have made his last stand, "and he shall come to his end, and there shall be none to help him" (see Isaiah 14:25; 30:31; 31:8, 9; Micah 5:5, 6).

3. THE KINGS OF THE EAST

When the sixth trumpet of the Apocalypse sounded, four angels who were held in bondage at the great river Euphrates were liberated to go forth and destroy a third of mankind (Revelation 9:13-15). When the sixth vial of wrath was poured out, it was upon the Euphrates with the result that the water was dried up that the way of the kings of the east might be prepared (Revelation 16:12).

The river Euphrates was the eastern boundary of the Roman Empire and formed a natural barrier between the east and the west. The difficulty of its passage was an effectual safeguard against invasion from the east. The drying up of its waters would leave the way wide open to the invader, and Revelation 9:16 implies that vast hordes of the eastern races, to the extent of two hundred millions, will pour into Palestine like the hordes of Ghengis Khan. What is portrayed in the inspired Word, however, is far more than a military expedition. A spiritual onslaught is also involved, and those who refuse to listen to the truth will evidently be tormented by lies and deception. The immense population of China, her clear desire for world domination and her need of land to provide food for her hungry people indicate how easily the prophecies may be fulfilled.

It seems evident that the Middle East is to be the cockpit of the world, with forces pouring in from every side and blood flowing like water. But it is equally clear that the coming of the Lord Jesus Christ in power and vengeance will betoken the destruction of all these mighty forces. He will crush His foes beneath His feet and free His people from all their fears.

4. THE ARAB POWERS

When British forces withdrew from Palestine in May, 1948, and left Israel to her fate, there seemed little hope of the survival of the new State, but to the amazement of the world, the little nation of 700,000 people routed the armies of the opposing nations of forty million Arabs. In 1956, Egypt, Syria and Jordan formed a unified army command for the purpose of war on Israel. The latter waited for no attack, but launched an assault on Sinai and destroyed two Egyptian divisions.

The Arabs seem completely convinced of their right to the land held by Israel, and there is every indication that perparations are being made for a third attack upon this small country. There is no doubt that a combined attack will eventually be made, and this may quite possibly take place after the removal of the church and before the institution of the millennium. In addition to all her other foes in a future day, it seems extremely probable that Israel will have to face the Arab nations as well. The Old Testament prophets make it abundantly plain, however, that judgment will fall upon the Arab people (Obadiah; Isaiah 34:5, 6; 63:1, ff.), and Ezekiel 36:5-9 reveals that the Arab will be swept out of the land and that Israel will be re-established there.

CHAPTER VIII. Babylon, The False Church

EARLY IN the world's history, a mighty hunter named Nimrod arose who determined to found a world empire, and Genesis 10:10 states that "the beginning of his kingdom was Babel." Nimrod, the son of Cush, has been identified by archaeologists with Bacchus, Tammuz and Adonis, and his wife, the beautiful Semiramis, was probably identical with the nature goddess Rhea or Cybele and also with Aphrodite of Greece and Venus of Rome. The fame of her beauty still lives in ancient history.

Nimrod was the first leader of human apostasy from God. All pagan mythologies and systems of idolatry show an underlying unity of character which indicates their common origin, and all may, in fact, be traced back to Babylon and its first ruler. Initially, he was regarded as a great benefactor, principally because of his exploits in the destruction of the wild beasts which threatened the world's relatively small population of his day. As a city-builder also, he provided protection from the savage animals of the field and forest, and men were glad to take advantage of the shelter thus afforded. Tradition declares that in addition he proceeded to emancipate men from the fear of God and the old patriarchal faith. The Noahic flood left the people with a dread of the Almighty and His judgments, but the Nimrodic apostasy delivered them from this fear and gained for their leader the title of "Deliverer".

The great rebel was cut off suddenly, being torn to pieces by a wild boar. Persian records reveal that after his death Nimrod was deified by his followers. The ancient world was well acquainted with the Edenic promise (Genesis 3:15) and rightly concluded that the bruising of the head of the woman's seed implied the death of the Deliverer. In brazen blasphemy Semiramis proclaimed that her husband was the promised seed, whose death had really been a voluntary sacrifice for the benefit of his partisans. This so fully accorded with the latter's inclinations that it was gladly accepted and worship was paid to the deified leader.

The worship of Nimrod, under various names, was for long practised only in secret and herein originated the ancient "mysteries". Egypt, Greece and Phoenicia all derived their religious systems and secret rites from the Babylonians. As A. Hyslop declares in *The Two Babylons*, the object of the mysteries was "to bind all mankind in blind and absolute submission to a hierarchy dependent on the sovereigns of Babylon." All knowledge was monopolized by the priesthood, and the king was the chief priest, or Pontifex Maximus. The Chaldeans believed in the transmigration of souls, and it was later accepted that Nimrod had reappeared as a posthumous son, supernaturally born by his widow, and it was not long before the worship of Nimrod had been replaced by the worship of the mother and the child. The cult of the queen of heaven and her babe, to quote Dr. Ironside, "became the mystery-religion of Phoenicia, and by the Phoenicians was carried to the ends of the earth. Ashtaroth and Tammuz became Isis and Horus in Egypt, Aphrodite and Eros in Greece, Venus and Cupid in Italy." When the gospel came to Egypt, the Babylonian goddess and her child were simply converted into the Virgin Mary and her Son. Idolatry thus originated with Babylon, and throughout Scripture the city stands as the symbol of false worship and idolatry.

Jeremiah 51 foretold the destruction of the city of Babylon

and declared that it should never rise again. Yet, when the Revelation is opened, Babylon reappears upon the scene. The Old Testament prophecies leave no future for the city, but the Apocalypse paints an idolatrous system of the same character as Babylon. A comparison of the last six chapters of Revelation shows that this idolatrous power is set in antithesis to another type. The great harlot of Revelation 17 is in contrast to the spotless bride of Revelation 19 and the idolatrous city of Revelation 18 is in contrast to the holy city of Revelation 21.

The Babylon of the Apocalypse is an apostate religious system, linked with Papal Rome but obviously having a wider significance than the Roman Catholic Church. When Babylon was captured by the Medes and Persians, the leaders of the ancient religious system fled to Pergamum, and the city became the headquarters of the old pagan religion, and the king of Pergamum became the Pontifex Maximus. When Attalus III, the king of Pergamum, died in 133 B.C., he bequeathed to the citizens of Rome his royal and priestly offices, his dominions and his great wealth. Subsequently, the Babylonian initiates migrated from Asia Minor to Italy, settling in the Etruscan plain, from whence they propagated the Etruscan Mysteries, which were precisely the same as those of the old cult. Eventually Rome became the center, and the Pontifex Maximus was established there. When Julius Caesar became the head of the State, he was elected Pontifex Maximus, and this title was held by each of the Roman emperors down to Gratian. The latter refused a title which made him the head of the State pagan religion, an in 378 A.D., Damasus, the then bishop of Rome, was appointed Pontifex Maximus and became not only the head of the church of Rome, but also the legitimate successor of the old Babylonian pontiffs, with his pontificate extending over the pagans. The College of Cardinals is the counterpart of the pagan college of pontiffs, deriving from the original council at Babylon. The worship of the queen of heaven and her son, purgatorial purification after death, holy water, priestly absolution, dedicated virgins, reservation of all knowledge to the priesthood, unification of political and religious control, and many another feature of the ancient Babylonian system have been taken over and assimilated by Papal Rome.

The vision of Babylon in Revelation 17 portrays her as a great harlot sitting upon a scarlet beast which had seven heads and ten horns and was "full of names of blasphemy." From the description given in the chapter, it is evident that the beast referred to is the western empire of Revelation 13. Riding upon the beast, the woman dominated the great apostate empire and was supported by its military and political might. Yet the true character of the beast is shown to be one of blatant and unashamed blasphemy. Arrayed in purple and scarlet (significantly the garments of popes and cardinals) and decked with gold and jewels, the woman held in her hand a golden cup full of her adulterous abominations and filthiness. As II Kings 23:13; Isaiah 44:19; Ezekiel 16:36, etc., indicate, abominations such as those which filled her cup are a symbol of idolatry. Rome's idolatry has always been productive of immorality, and the filth which filled the cup is comprised of all her encouragements to sin — indulgences, enforced celibacy, auricular confession, conventual life and so on.

As the common prostitute in olden times wore her name on her brow, so a name was impressed upon the forehead of the great whore: "Mystery, Babylon the Great, the mother of harlots and of the abominations of the earth." She is said to sit upon seven mountains and is finally identified in Revelation 17:18 as the great city, which has kingship over the kings of the earth. Quite clearly, what is portrayed is a tremendous religious system, exercising authority over the political power, having its headquarters at Rome but being much larger in scope than Roman Catholicism since the woman is "the mother of harlots." The one-world church, for which so many are striving today, will inevitably be achieved in the future, but it is significant that the headquarters will remain at Rome. Reunion with Rome will be on Rome's terms, and she is unlikely to offer any compromise.

The universal church of the future will evidently be in such close co-operation with the political power that her will is dominant and her supreme authority is acknowledged throughout the empire. Such a close association will surely have a considerable effect in binding the countries together in loyalty to the leader approved so wholeheartedly by the church. The official recognition of the authority of the church will cease when the western emperor claims Divine homage and worship. With the setting up of his image in the temple at Jerusalem and his decree that all worship should be paid to him alone, the links with the ecclesiastical power will be rudely broken. There will possibly be other contributory factors. Obviously the church will not tolerate the rival claims made by the emperor, but additionally the constantly increasing wealth of the church will attract criticism. The western ruler and his satellite powers will apparently become restive under the church's intolerant sway, and coveting her wealth, will turn upon her and strip her of her wealth and treasures. Just as Henry VIII plundered the English churches and monasteries, so will this later church suffer spoliation and destruction at the hand of the political power. It seems only fitting that the end of the great religious system should be due to the very powers which allowed her to exercise despotic control over the lives of their subjects.

Revelation 18 discloses that the fall of Babylon will have far-reaching effects. The vast commercial and economic system, which has brought — and will yet bring — nations and kingdoms into its toils, will suddenly collapse without warning. So complete will be its destruction that the Apocalypse depicts it as a mighty conflagration which strikes fear into the hearts of the spectators. From every quarter will rise the wails from those whose temporal prosperity has been destroyed. The details given show plainly that Babylon will be the personification of the commercial spirit as well as of the ecclesiastical, and there are already confirmatory evidences of this. The future of the one-world church, as portrayed in Scripture, may be summed up as a sudden rise to power followed by an equally sudden fall. It is a false church and a mere counterfeit of the true.

 # The Prince of Darkness

THE APPARENT existence of two conflicting principles in nature early gave rise to what Reville termed, "an eminently dualistic conception of the forces or divinities which direct the course of events," and this really lies at the root of the dualism which is inherent in all forms of nature worship. During the captivity, the Israelites were brought into contact with the teaching of Persian Zoroastrianism — which had the same basic features — and it has often been suggested that it was in the mythological conflict of the evil Ahriman with the good Ormuz that the doctrine of a personal devil first found its origin. It is quite plain that neither pagan conceptions nor mythology formed the basis of the Biblical doctrine, however, for the Scriptures had clearly referred to the existence of this mighty being at a much earlier date.

It is sometimes maintained that the devil is merely a personification of the principle of evil and is not an actual being, but this is plainly irreconcilable with the teachings of Scripture (Matthew 13:39; John 13:2; Acts 5:3; I Peter 5:8). "The personal existence of a spirit of evil," says Barry, "is revealed again and again in Scripture. Every quality, every action, which can indicate personality, is attributed to him in language which cannot be explained away." He is capable of movement (Job 1:7, 12), he enters into men (John 13:27), he lays snares for them (I Timothy 3:7; II Timothy 2:26), he tempted Christ (Matthew 4: 1-9), he is described by our Lord as a liar and murderer while activities and characteristics are credited to him which can only be applicable to a person. If our Lord's testimony is to be accepted, there is no question as to the personality of Satan. Findlay says, "In the visible forms of sin, Jesus saw the shadow of His great antagonist. From the Evil One He taught His disciples to pray that they might be delivered. The victims of disease and madness whom He healed were so many captives rescued from the malignant power of Satan. And when Jesus went to meet His death, He viewed it as the supreme conflict with the usurper and oppressor who claimed to be 'the prince of this world.' "

Satan is neither self-existent nor eternal. He is a created being and came into existence by the hand of God. In his first estate, he was one of the cherubim of the highest angelic order and standing in closest proximity to God Himself. He was "the anointed covering (or protecting) cherub" (Ezekiel 28:14). "Like the golden cherubim, covering the visible mercy-seat in the holy of holies of the earthly tabernacle," writes Chafer, "he was created a guard and covering cherub to the heavenly center of glory."

Ezekiel's "lamentation" upon the King of Tyre (Ezekiel 28:12-15), although addressed to an earthly potentate, obviously goes beyond the earthly king and applies to one of greater power — even to Satan himself — the real, though unseen, ruler of Tyre. The prophecy reveals that this mighty spirit was created by God for immediate attendance upon Himself and that he was placed in a position of close relationship to His throne, being connected as one of the cherubim, with the holiness and governmental purposes of the Almighty. From the day of his creation, he received honour and dignity and was in "Eden, the garden of God," not the Adamic Eden, but as Torrey suggests, "an earlier one. The Adamic Eden was remarkable for its vegetable glory. This early Eden for its mineral glory. Compare the New Jerusalem (Revelation 21:10-21). In the Adamic Eden, Satan was present, not as here, as a minister of God, but as an apostate spirit and a tempter. The glory of the early Eden seems to have been specially prepared for Satan. There was also the pomp of royalty, tabrets and pipes."

Surpassing all other created beings in his marvellous beauty, it is recorded that he was "perfect in beauty;" taught by the Almighty, he possessed divinely-given wisdom; cherished and honoured above all created intelligences, he was the anointed covering cherub, dwelling in the mountain of God, walking in the midst of the stones of fire and possessing the mark of God's approval in a covering of gold and precious stones. From the reference to musical instruments and to his anointing, it has sometimes been deduced that he was also connected with the worship of the angelic hosts and that he was possibly the leader in this service. Set in authority in the midst of the heavens, it is possible that the whole hierarchy of angels was in subjection to him, but little is recorded of the extent of the original power of the great Lucifer.

The recipient of such blessing and favour might have been expected to exhibit the utmost loyalty to his benefactor, but an inordinate pride and overweening ambition led to his tragic fall (I Timothy 3:6). In amazing arrogance, he sought the supreme place in heaven. Whether he endeavoured to divert the worship of the angelic hosts from the Creator to himself, or whether he put himself at the head of a rebellious army of angels in heaven in a desperate attempt to overthrow God and to establish himself on the throne of the Almighty, is not explicitly revealed. But, with the dejected hosts of his followers, he was expelled from the immediate presence of God and deprived of his glory and dignity. "Thou was perfect in thy ways

. . . till iniquity was found in thee," declared Ezekiel. ". . . thou hast sinned: therefore have I cast thee as profane out of the mountain of God: and I will destroy thee, O covering cherub, from the midst of the stones of fire" (Ezekiel 28:15, 16). Isaiah gives a further glimpse of that dark hour when he writes, "How art thou fallen from heaven, O Lucifer, son of the morning! . . . For thou hadst said in thine heart, I will ascend into heaven, I will exalt my throne above the stars of God: I will sit also upon the mount of the congregation in the sides of the north: I will ascend above the heights of the clouds; I will be like the Most High: yet thou shalt be brought down to hell, to the sides of the pit" (Isaiah 14:12-15). The devil was the original sinner (I John 3:8) and a bitter price has he already paid for that act of sin.

Deprived of his former estate, Satan became not only the author of sin but the great arch-enemy of truth and holiness, and the title he will carry into the lake of fire — "that old deceiver, the devil" — will perpetuate the memory of his iniquity and the origin of sin.

Some of the angels who fell with him were divinely seized and imprisoned in chains to await the execution of the judgment which will cast them with their leader into the lake of fire (II Peter 2:4, 5; Jude 6). Satan evidently has a greater liberty than his former satellites but has been appointed well-defined limits beyond which he cannot go.

From the moment of his downfall, Satan set himself in opposition to God and sought particularly to frustrate the divine purposes in relation to man. To unfallen man in the garden of Eden, he appeared in the guise of a serpent and enticed to a deliberate transgression of the commandment of God (Genesis 3:4-7). In the antediluvian period there seems to have been an unprecedented demonstration of Satanic activity ("the sons of God" in Genesis 6:2 seem to have been fallen angels who left their proper estate — although it is suggested by some that they were descendants of Seth). He tempted David to number Israel (I Chronicles 21:1). He consistently attacks God's people today and attempts to seduce them from the path of loyalty to Christ.

His efforts were particularly directed against the Messiah, however. When Adam fell God revealed that a Redeemer would come; the Seed of the woman should bruise the serpent's head, and he should bruise His heel (Genesis 3:15). From that moment commenced a long-drawn-out struggle on Satan's part to prevent the fulfillment of the promise. The murder of Abel (Genesis 4:8), the universal corruption and consequent judgment of Noah's day (Genesis 6), the murder of the Hebrew babes (Exodus 1:16), are all illustrations of his attempts to blot out the line through which the Redeemer should come. In the time of Athaliah, an attempt was made to destroy the whole of the royal house, and it was only through the intervention of his aunt, Jehoshabeath, and the fidelity of Jehoida, the priest, that the sole survivor, Josiah, was preserved (II Chronicles 22:10-12).

When the forerunner of the Messiah appeared in the person of John the Baptist as foretold by Isaiah and Malachi, prophecy had prepared the devil for the Coming One Himself. Hence his instigation of Herod to destroy the children of Bethlehem (Matthew 2:16).

When our Lord was about to enter upon His public ministry, Satan took the step of personally assailing Him in the severest of temptations to entice Him to sacrifice the object of His incarnation. Suffering from the pangs of hunger, Christ was tempted to satisfy the appetite by a miracle. From the pinnacle of the temple, the tempter urged Him to show His power and majesty by a miraculous descent. Arraying all the kingdoms of the world before Him, Satan offered Him all their glory and sovereignty in return for His swerving from the path of allegiance to God (Matthew 4: 1-10). But every temptation was completely unavailing.

In due time, however, the Lamb of God was delivered

into the hands of those who sought His life. In order to ensure the achievement of his purpose, Satan entered into Judas Iscariot (Luke 22:3) and inspired the man of Kerioth in his treacherous betrayal. The subsequent agony of Calvary told something of the devil's power, and the Psalmist reveals the depths of Satanic malignity; even in those moments of untold suffering, the forces of evil gathered exultantly around the Cross. "Great bulls have compassed Me; Bashan's strong ones have beset Me round, . . . Dogs have encompassed Me; an assembly of evil-doers have surrounded Me" (Psalm 22:12, 16). What transpired during those hours of darkness we may never fully know.

In that hour of Satan's greatest victory, the Christ of God turned defeat into victory. He undid the works of the devil (I John 3:8), annulled his power (Hebrews 2:14) and defeated him who had the power of death. From the depths of Hades Christ released the souls of the blest, and wresting from the devil the keys of death and Hades, He rose triumphantly on the third day, carrying back with Him a multitude of captives (Ephesians 4:8; Hebrews 2:14, 15). He spoiled the Satanic principalities and authorities and made an open show of His triumph over them (Colossians 2:15). The first great blow towards the complete bruising of the serpent's head had been struck; the bruising of the heel of the woman's Seed had been fulfilled at Calvary, and the final crushing of the evil one was now assured.

Despite his fall, Satan has not yet been deprived of all his dignity. Indeed, so exalted is his position still that even Michael the archangel, "did not dare to bring a railing judgment against Him" (Jude 9).

He is still "the ruler of the authority of the air" (Ephesians 2:2). The Jewish rabbis taught that the terrestrial atmosphere was his abode and that it was peopled with spirit beings. This is supported by the apostle's statement, "our struggle is not against flesh and blood, but against principalities, against authorities, against the universal lords of this darkness, against spiritual powers of wickedness in the heavenlies" (Ephesians 6:12). Satan is the sovereign of hosts of evil spirits who make their abode in the physical atmosphere. Our Lord specifically used the title Beelzebub, the chief of the demons, of him (Luke 11:18, 19).

The devil is also described as "the prince of this world," and our Lord recognized his right to this title (John 12: 31; 14:30; 16:11). "Was this world a department assigned to him of God as separate kingdoms have been assigned to different celestial potentates?" asks Torrey. "Did he drag down his dominion with him in his own fall?" It is sometimes suggested that this earth was the scene of his former glory and that it suffered a pre-Adamite judgment as a result of his fall, and some colour is given to this by references in Isaiah and Jeremiah (Isaiah 24:1; Jeremiah 4: 23; c.f., Genesis 1:2 with Isaiah 45:18).

Whether this is so or not, evidences are not wanting that spiritual as well as human powers are concerned with the administration of the earth. Isaiah, for example, declares that in a coming day God, "will punish the host of the high ones on high, and the kings of the earth upon the earth" (Isaiah 24:21), i.e., both the spiritual and the human rulers. Again, when the angel of the Lord came forth to speak with Daniel, he was confronted by rebel spirit princes, whose titles indicated their terrestrial authority (Daniel 10:21). Satan evidently still has authority and, as Pember has said, "divides the world into different provinces according to its nationalities, appointing a powerful angel, assisted directly by countless subordinates, as viceroy over each kingdom."

"The powers that be are ordained of God," but within the restrictions set him by the Almighty, Satan is behind the whole system of world government, and powers are but puppets in his hand. He exercises all the rights of sovereignty in a scene which so readily subjects itself to him. The greed and ambition of the nations, the diplomacy and deceit of the political world, the bitter hatred and rivalry in the sphere of commerce, and the organization of many forms of government itself proceed from a Satanic source. It was this sovereignty that he offered to Christ (Luke 4:6), and his right to offer it was not disputed by our Lord. "Though under the restraining hand of God," says Chafer, "Satan is now in authority over the unregenerate world, and the unsaved are unconsciously organized and federated under his leading. . . . This federation includes all of the unsaved and fallen humanity; it has the co-operation of the fallen spirits, and is but the union of all who are living and acting in independence of God." The Satanic system is utterly evil and at enmity with God (James 4:4). It is corrupt (II Peter 1:4) and polluted (II Peter 2:20). "The whole world lies in the wicked one" (I John 5:19). With the exception of the redeemed, the entire mass of men rests supinely in the devil's embrace. The death-knell of that mighty dominion was sounded, however, at Calvary (John 12:31).

The cause of Satan's original downfall was a desire to be on an equality with God, and that deep-seated ambition is still buried in his heart. Not content with the rule of men's ways, he seeks supremacy over their hearts and cleverly directs the religious worship of mankind to himself. "The god of this age," wrote Paul, "has blinded the thoughts of the unbelieving" (II Corinthians 4:4). In order that the glory of the gospel might not shine into their hearts, Satan presents himself to their gaze. To some he becomes the great Mammon, the god of money; to others he takes the form of the Muses or Arts; others worship him as fame or fortune, or even as the personification of religion. Through each channel, by every idol he sets up, he gains the worship of a section of the inhabitants of the world, blinding them to the light of the gospel. Behind every phase and facet of man's objects of worship is the central figure of the "god of this age."

The early Christians believed that evil spirits were behind all the deities of the ancient pantheons, and that all worship of false gods was, therefore, ultimately directed to Satan. This belief was confirmed by the apostle Paul when he wrote, "What the nations sacrifice, they sacrifice to demons and not to God" (I Corinthians 10:20). Even today it is impossible, as one writer remarks, "to explain all occult phenomena and phrenetic moral aberrations by physical causes," and there is little doubt that behind the idols of the heathen are the spiritual forces of Satan.

During the present day, the devil has power over the physical bodies of unbelievers (Luke 13:16; Acts 10:38) and where permitted by God, can also inflict malady and physical suffering even upon believers (Job 1:9-12; I Corinthians 5:5; II Corinthians 12:7). He had formerly "the might of death" (Hebrews 2:14), (i.e., authority in the realms of death), but the Son of God, descending into death, defeated him and rose again triumphantly.

Throughout this present age, Satan is permitted to have a part in the sifting and testing of believers (Luke 22:31), but the Lord is ever watching and ready to supply all needed help in the hour of temptation. Indeed, the testings are often divinely permitted in order that faith may be proved. While he is engaged on earth, the devil also finds an access before God to draw attention to the faults and failings of those who seek to live godly lives (Job 1: 6-12; 2:1-7). The day is not far distant, however, when he will be ejected for ever from that heavenly sphere (Revelation 12:9, 10).

Although his power is so great, Satan suffers from restrictions placed upon Him by God. His power, through his demon and angel forces, is almost beyond comprehension, but the power of God is greater than all the forces of the evil one, and Paul declares that not even angels, principalities or powers shall separate the Christian from the love of God (Romans 8:38, 39). Satan's limitations are clearly indicated in Scripture. Although his evil hosts make his power felt throughout the world, he is not omnipotent since, as in the case of Job, he has to seek divine permission before he may inflict suffering on God's people. Despite his unparalleled intelligence, he is not omniscient as is apparent from the many errors he has made in history, particularly in his dealings with Christ. Nor is he omnipresent as he revealed in his statement in Job's day that he came, "from going to and fro in the earth, and from walking up and down in it" (Job 1:7; 2:2).

With the myriads of his spirit hosts, Satan possesses a power which might well cause men to quail in fear were it not for the fact that his power is at present held in check by the restraining influence of the Holy Spirit and the church of God (II Thessalonians 2:6, 7). At the coming of Christ to the air, however, the Holy Spirit and the church He indwells will be removed (I Thessalonians 4:15-17; I Corinthians 15:51-54), and the devil will be at liberty to produce his masterpiece — a complete travesty of divine things. In place of the church he will present to the world a great counterfeit, Babylon the harlot (Revelation 17); in the stead of Christ he will introduce Antichrist (II Thessalonians 2); and in lieu of God's King he will enthrone the Beast (Revelation 13:1-10).

His access to the heavenlies will be taken from him, and after bitter warfare with Michael and his angels, he will be cast down to the earth (Revelation 12:7-12). His days of liberty numbered, Satan's fury will be unleashed, but when wickedness has reached its culmination, the Son of Man will appear in glory with the hosts of His saints to execute judgment upon all (Jude 14). The armies of Satan's two puppets will be destroyed, the leaders taken and cast alive into the lake of fire (Revelation 19:11-21), while the devil, who inspired them, will be judicially bound and sealed in the abyss there to remain impotent for 1,000 years (Revelation 20:1-3).

Throughout the millennium, Satan will necessarily be inactive, but at its close he will again be loosed for "a little season" (Revelation 20:7). Unchanged in character, his undeviating purpose will remain the frustration of God's will. With bitter hatred he will use his liberty to organize a last desperate attempt to overthrow the Almighty, gathering together all the forces of evil and all the nations of the earth against the beloved city. Inspired by their mighty leader, the great armies will seek to make war on the Lamb and the saints only to find bitter retribution in consuming fire from heaven (Romans 20:9). His plans dissolved and his power forever broken, Satan will be powerless before God who will pronounce his eternal, irrevocable doom. Once the anointed cherub and favoured one of God, he will be cast into the lake of fire long reserved for him (Matthew 25:41), to be tormented day and night for ever and ever (Revelation 20:10).

(A fuller discussion of this subject will be found in the author's book *The Prince of Darkness*).

 # The Day
of the Lord

Writing about 800 b.c., the prophet Joel described the experience of the southern kingdom of Judah at the hands of God. The people had ignored the claims of Jehovah, had paid no regard to His laws and had withheld the sacrifices which should have been brought to the temple. Eventually His wrath fell upon them, and they were scourged by a visitation of locusts of unparalleled severity. In addition to the complete devastation of the land, the plague was evidently accompanied by a severe drought, and all means of subsistence disappeared. The prophet called upon Judah to repent and to turn to the Lord in contrition, for if they did not, "the day of the Lord" was at hand and would come as a destruction from the Almighty (Joel 1:15). What the people had suffered was without precedent in their experience, but the day of the Lord was one of clouds and thick darkness before which they might justifiably tremble (Joel 2:1, 2).

Despite the opportunity afforded for repentance, God knew perfectly well that once the cause of their troubles was removed and their fear dispelled, all signs of penitence would disappear and the people would revert to their impious backsliding. Having warned them thus briefly of the dread day of the Lord, He revealed that a still more awful period lay ahead which the prophet described as "the great and terrible day of the Lord" (Joel 2:31). In the third chapter of his book, Joel gives further details of this second outpouring of judgment and reveals that it will be completely cataclysmic, involving both heaven and earth, and also that it will be related to the gathering of the nations of the earth against Jerusalem immediately prior to a divine interposition from heaven. Then the Lord will, "roar out of Zion and utter His voice from Jerusalem," and in the shaking of the universe will prove Himself the hope and strength of His people (Joel 3:16).

A few years later, the northern kingdom of Israel received an inspired message through the prophet Amos regarding their own circumstances. Divine retribution had fallen upon them because of their sin and backsliding, and they had suffered a succession of attacks from their hostile neighbors. In desperation, some had expressed a longing for the day of the Lord, obviously intending thereby an intervention by God on their behalf to defend them against the hostile nations surrounding them. But they had not realized the implication of their words, and the prophet explained that the day of the Lord is darkness and not light (Amos 5:18), in other words, judgment rather than deliverance. God would indeed intervene, but not in the way they had hoped. They had not listened to His pleas or expostulations, and He would accordingly deliver them into captivity beyond Damascus and implied that they should realize that this very intervention was a reminder of the still future judgments of the day of the Lord.

A decade or two later, the prophet Isaiah warned the people that before God ushered in the universal peace and blessing so long hoped for, the day of the Lord would come. "Enter into the rock," cried the prophet, "and hide thee in the dust, from before the terror of the Lord, and from the glory of His majesty . . . for the day of the Lord of hosts shall be upon everyone that is proud and lofty, and upon everyone that is lifted up . . . and they shall go into the holes of the rocks and into the caves of the earth, for fear of the Lord, and for the glory of His majesty, when He ariseth to shake terribly the earth" (Isaiah 2:10-19).

Confirming the predictions of the earlier prophets, Isaiah also foretold the second cataclysm following the continued disobedience of the people. That awful period would be "the day of the Lord's vengeance, and the year of recompenses for the controversy of Zion." The stars of heaven would be dissolved and the heavens rolled up like a scroll (Isaiah 34:1-8).

A further revelation was given in Isaiah 61:1-6, where the inspired writer set the day of God's vengeance between our Lord's life on earth and the future establishment of the millennial kingdom. It is significant that when our Lord read these words in the synagogue at Nazareth on that memorable sabbath day, He stopped in the middle of verse 2, omitting the reference to the day of God's vengeance, and declared of the earlier clauses of verses 1 and 2, "This day is this Scripture fulfilled in your ears" (Luke 4:19-21), clearly indicating that the day of judgment was still to come.

Many another quotation from the Old Testament prophets might be made, but Jeremiah makes it clear that the Divine judgment will be inflicted primarily upon God's earthly people. After indicating the awfulness of that day, he specifically related it to Israel when he described it as "the time of Jacob's trouble" (Jeremiah 30:7). This is implicitly confirmed in Daniel 12:1 (see also Deuteronomy 4:29), but both prophets also imply that God's people shall eventually be saved.

When we come to the New Testament, there are again indications that Israel's day of trouble still awaits her. It is also plain from our Lord's words in Matthew 24:29, 30 and Luke 21:25-27 that in addition the more awful cataclysmic period described by the prophets — when the sky will be darkened and the celestial bodies will be affected — will occur immediately after a period described as "the tribulation" (i.e., the period of Israel's trouble) and that it will culminate in the Second Advent of Christ in power and glory.

In his second epistle, the apostle Peter states, "the day of the Lord will come as a thief in the night," and that it will be accompanied by the dissolution of the earth and the heavens (II Peter 3:10). Whether or not the apostle intended to refer in this verse to the second stage of the day of the Lord to which we have already referred, in the succeeding verses (12 and 13) he certainly looked on to an even later period, which he described as "the day of God", when the existing heavens and earth will be superseded by new heavens and a new earth.

From the Scriptures quoted, it will be evident that the day of the Lord covers a long period, apparently concluding with the end of time and the preparation for the eternal state. It also seems reasonably clear that it has at least two — and possibly three — stages. But when does it actually commence?

In II Thessalonians 2:2-4, the apostle Paul states that the day of the Lord (not the day of *Christ* as in the A.V.) cannot come, ". . . except there come a falling away (or apostasy) first, and that man of sin be revealed, the son of perdition; who opposeth and exalteth himself above all that is called God, or that is worshipped; so that he as God, sitteth in the temple of God, showing himself that he is God." In Mark 13:14-19, our Lord (referring to the same event) warned the godly who would be in Judea at the time that when they saw, "the abomination of desolation spoken of by Daniel the prophet standing where *he* (not *it* as in the A.V.) ought not," they should flee to the mountains, for unprecedented affliction would then be the experience of the people. In fact, so awful would be the time that, unless the days were shortened, no flesh would be saved. Daniel 9:27 indicates that this event will happen in the middle of the seventieth "week" of that prophecy, and this is possibly confirmed by Revelation 12:14, in which the godly remnant of Israel, symbolized as a woman, flee from the devil's persecutions to a hiding place in the wilderness for three and one-half years (see also Daniel 7:25; 12:7).

Malachi 4:5 states, "before the great and terrible day of the Lord come," God will send Elijah the prophet. On the basis of this statement, it has been argued by many that either Elijah personally, or another whom he typified, must be one of the two witnesses referred to in Revelation 11:3. These two men are to prophesy — apparently in Jerusalem — for 1260 days (i.e., on the basis of a 360 day year, three and one-half years). Since the day of the Lord cannot come before the expiry of their witness of three and one-half years, and since the period of Israel's persecution is to last three and one-half years, it is evident that the commencement must be in the middle of Daniel's seventieth heptad.

The day of the Lord (and the great tribulation which forms a part of the whole period) has no reference, of course, to the church. It is the period of God's wrath, but as the apostle Paul points out in I Thessalonians 5:5, 9, *we* are not of the night and God has not appointed *us* to wrath. On the other hand, he specifically states in verse 3, "sudden destruction cometh upon *them* . . . and *they* shall not escape," obviously distinguishing between believers and unbelievers. As already mentioned in Chapter IV, the seventieth week of Daniel 9 cannot commence before the removal of the church, and clearly, therefore, the events of the second half of that week cannot be of concern to the church or the Christian.

The consistent picture given of the day of the Lord in Scripture is of a period, starting suddenly and unexpectedly, coming "as a thief in the night" (I Thessalonians 5:1, 2) and characterized by Divine wrath and judgment. Associated with it are signs in the heavens, such as the darkening of the sun, moon and constellations, and calamitous events upon earth, graphically described in the Apocalypse. It seems evident that it will be a time of unexampled trouble for Israel and that she will then suffer Divine retribution for her sins. But the judgments of Revelation 6 to 16 patently go far beyond Israel and affect the whole world. J. F. Strombeck has given the following excellent summary in *First the Rapture*:

"1. It shall come with unexpected suddenness upon the dwellers on the earth at a time 'when they shall say, Peace and safety' — a time of false security.

2. That day shall come as a destruction from the Lord, and as a devouring fire. It shall be a day of trouble and distress. It is the day of wrath and fierce anger and of the Lord's vengeance.

3. It shall be a day of clouds, a day of gloom and darkness, even thick darkness. The stars of heaven and the constellations thereof shall not give their light. The sun shall be darkened and the moon turned to blood. The heavens and the earth shall be shaken and the earth removed out of her place.

4. The indignation of the Lord shall be upon all people. The Lord shall punish the world for their evil and the wicked for their iniquity. He shall bring distress upon men because they have sinned against Him.

5. The day of the Lord shall be the day of Jacob's trouble. Sinners of Israel shall be destroyed out of the land. It shall be a day of purging before the Son of Man comes in the clouds of heaven.

6. But deliverance shall come to Mount Zion and Jerusalem to the remnant of Israel. The Lord shall be the hope of His people and the strength of Israel. Their land shall be blessed and the house of Jacob shall possess their possessions.

7. Israel shall see Him whom they have pierced and mourn as one mourneth for the only son. Unto those who fear His name shall the Sun of righteousness appear with healing under His wings. The feet of the Lord shall stand

upon the Mount of Olives, and living waters shall go out from Jerusalem. Jesus said that, after the tribulation, the Son of Man shall come in the clouds of heaven with power and great glory. Then the Messianic kingdom shall be established and the Lord shall be king over all the earth."

The day of the Lord is a long period, commencing at the setting up of the image of the western emperor in the temple at Jerusalem and covering the ensuing three and one-half years of the great tribulation, when Israel will suffer as never before, enduring the judgments of God and the attacks of the nations. It will cover also the outpouring of Divine wrath upon the godless peoples of earth at the glorious coming of Christ. The long beneficent rule of the millennium which He will then introduce will be but a parenthetical age, and the final rebellion at its close will lead to a further intervention from heaven when the fire of God will fall upon the rebellious hosts (Revelation 20:9). The last act of judgment will embrace this planet and its atmosphere in nuclear destruction (II Peter 3:10) — the final event in the day of the Lord before eternal peace and tranquility are ushered in.

 # The King's Advent

IMMEDIATELY AFTER the nuptial bliss and joy of the Lamb's marriage supper (Revelation 19:7), the Apocalypse declares that the heaven will open and the Almighty Conqueror will ride forth in all His glory to judge and make war. He will come to smite the nations with the sword and to rule over them with an iron rod. The One with flaming eyes and diademed head and bloody garment, "treads the winepress of the fury of the wrath of Almighty God" (Revelation 19:11-16). He rides forth on a white horse, and cohorts of white-robed believers follow Him on white horses. This is the day of which Enoch prophesied, "Behold, the Lord cometh with ten thousands of His saints, to execute judgment upon all . . ." (Jude 14, 15). In relentless fury the Divine wrath is to be poured out upon the unregenerate and vengeance to be satiated in their doom. For centuries the Spirit of God has striven with men and sought their repentance and salvation. The invitation to the feast has been offered repeatedly, but the blind and insensate race has refused to heed the call. In that day of wrath, the tables will be turned, and those who had been invited to the feast will themselves become a feast for the ravening birds. The bodies of kings, captains, mighty men, freemen and slaves will lie unburied on the battlefield, the food of the gathering vultures (Revelation 19:17, 18). Zechariah declares that the Lord shall go forth to fight against the nations (Zechariah 14:3), and He will utterly destroy.

The picture that is painted is unquestionably of a literal

advent of Christ "in the clouds of heaven with power and great glory" (Matthew 24:30), as He Himself foretold. The prophet discloses that He will descend to Olivet and that the mountain will cleave in two at the impact and that a great valley will appear, through which the waters will flow from the Mediterranean into the Dead Sea (Zechariah 14: 4-8). When He comes, it will be to find the armies of the western empire arrayed against the faithful in Israel, but the great leader of the west and his Jewish satellite, the false prophet, will be ruthlessly snatched from the scene and cast for ever into the lake of fire while their tremendous forces become the prey of the feathered hosts (Revelation 19:18-21). The immense armies from the east will simultaneously meet with their end at Megiddo (Revelation 16:12-21). The arm of the Lord will be made bare.

Prior to our Lord's advent, the forces of the south will have been defeated by the northern power. As the latter is overrunning Egypt, however, tidings from the north-east will reach him, telling of startling events in Israel which provoke him into instant activity. As already described in Chapter VII, the infuriated northerner will turn back to destroy Israel's Deliverer and to crush the people beneath his feet. But it is he and his forces who will be utterly destroyed, and none shall rise to help them (Daniel 11: 40-45).

The mighty Conqueror will come in invincible power to destroy the enemies of His people, and it is difficult to picture that awful period. Seiss writes, "The great Conquerer bows the heavens and comes down. He rides upon the cherub horse, and flies upon the wings of the wind. Smoke goes up from His nostrils, and devouring fire out of His mouth. He moves amid storms and darkness, from which lightnings hurl their bolts, and hailstones mingle with the fire. He roars out of Zion and utters His voice from Jerusalem, till the heavens and the earth shake. He dashes forth in the fury of His incensed greatness amid clouds and fire and pillars of smoke. The sun frowns. The day is neither light nor dark. The mountains melt and cleave asunder at His presence. The hills bound from their seats and skip like lambs. The waters are dislodged from their channels. The sea rolls back with howling trepidation. The sky is rent and folds back upon itself like a collapsed tent. It is the day for executing an armed world — a world in covenant with hell to overthrow the authority and throne of God — and everything in terrified Nature joins to signalize the deserved vengeance. So the Scriptures everywhere represent." In view of the events taking place and the fact that it is the eternal God who has come forth to this tiny planet, one can well appreciate that some of the expressions of prophecy are no mere imagery but are intended to convey a vivid impression of actual occurrences. Should not the heavens shake and the earth tremble and the stars be affected when the Eternal Himself intervenes?

Every eye shall see our Lord in that day, and the peoples will wail because of Him (Revelation 1:7), for He then comes to judge the living (Acts 10:42; II Timothy 4:1; Psalm 96:13). In the days of His flesh, He disclosed that at His appearing in glory with all His holy angels, He would "sit upon the throne of His glory" and that all the living peoples would be brought before Him for judgment (Matthew 25:31-46). In solemn silence He will take His seat as described in Daniel 7:9, 10, and the world of the living will be gathered to this assize on earth. During the years preceding, Jewish preachers throughout the world will have proclaimed to the nations the gospel of the coming King (Matthew 24:14), and multitudes of Gentiles will apparently turn to God for salvation (Revelation 7:9, 10). "They manifest the genuineness of their faith by works," says A. C. Gaebelein (*The Gospel According to Matthew*). "The preachers who are going about are persecuted and hated by others, suffering, hungry and some cast into prison. These nations who believe their testimony show their faith by giving them to eat, clothing them, visiting them in prison and by showing love to them. . . . Grace thus covers them because they believed."

It might perhaps be deduced from Matthew 25 that the living are judged solely on the basis of their treatment of the Jewish nation, but eternal bliss or eternal suffering would scarcely be meted out on that basis. As J. D. Pentecost writes in *Things to Come,* "This judgment must be a judgment to determine the spiritual condition of those being judged. It is to determine whether the one judged is saved or unsaved. A casual glance at the passage seems to show that this is a judgment based on works, with the outcome depending on the works of the one judged. A closer observation will not support this conclusion. First of all, it is the accepted principle in Scripture that a man is never saved by works, for nowhere is salvation offered on a works basis. In Matthew 25:46 it says, 'And these shall go away into everlasting punishment: but the righteous into life eternal.' We thus see that the eternal destiny of the people appearing before the judgment was being decided. It could not be a judgment of works, for eternal destiny is never decided on that basis, but on the basis of the acceptance or rejection of Christ's work for us. Further, those that had fed, given to drink, clothed, and visited the 'brethren' were called righteous. If this is a judgment of works, they must have been constituted as righteous on the basis of what they had done. Such would be contrary to the teaching of Scripture."

As the living assemble before the throne of Christ, He will divide them, as a shepherd divides the sheep from the goats, placing the "sheep" on His right hand and the "goats" on His left. Those on His right hand are to be brought into the blessings of the millennial kingdom which He is about to introduce. "Inasmuch as ye have done it unto one of the least of these My brethren (i.e., the Jews), ye have done it unto Me," are the words of the Master. Those who have been regenerated by the Holy Spirit through faith in the gospel of the kingdom will have been prepared to risk martyrdom to help God's people, thus demonstrating the reality of their faith. Accordingly these Gentile believers will enter into everlasting bliss. To those on the left hand, the Judge's words are equally explicit, "Inasmuch as ye did it not to one of the least of these (i.e., the Jews), ye did it not to Me." These people knew not God; they had exercised no faith in the gospel which had been preached to them. Their attitude to our Lord's Jewish brethren was, therefore, actuated by hatred instead of love. On these Christ will pass the awful sentence, "Depart from Me . . . into everlasting fire." This is no mere exclusion from the earthly kingdom; it is a permanent and irrevocable judgment. These people are rejectors of God and His gospel, and they will have sealed their own doom.

The judgment of the living nations, as described in Matthew 25, is not synonymous, of course, with the final assize of the great white throne referred to in Revelation 20. The first will take place immediately prior to the millennium; and the latter will not take place until after the millennium and the dissolution of the earth. The first is concerned with all those who are alive at the Second Advent of Christ; the other will deal with all the dead and those who did not stand at the earthly tribunal.

Before the kingdom is instituted, the nation of Israel must also be brought into judgment. Not all Jews of that day will have put their trust in God, "For they are not all Israel, which are of Israel" (Romans 9:6). Only those who have been regenerated by the Holy Spirit will be eligible to enter the kingdom. Ezekiel declares that the Lord will bring Israel out of the countries in which they are scattered and bring them into the wilderness (presumably on the borders of the land) to be dealt with. There He will purge out the rebels and transgressors and exclude them from the land of Israel (Ezekiel 20:34-38). A later prophet shows that the Judge will discern the character of the evil-doer and will cast him out (Malachi 3:2-5). Their spiritual condition will be revealed by their actions and habits, and the unsaved will be separated from the saved, and "the unprofitable servant" will be cast into outer darkness" (Matthew 25:30). As in the case of the Gentiles, the judgment is, of course, restricted to the living and is not concerned with the dead. That the latter are not forgotten is evident from Isaiah 26:19 and Daniel 12:2, 3, from which it is plain that the saved of Israel's seed are raised for blessing and the unsaved left for the final assize. N. West in *The Thousand Years in Both Testaments* explains, "the true rendering of Daniel 12:2, 3, in connection with the context, is 'and (at that time) many (of thy people) shall awake (or be separated) out from among the sleepers in the earth dust. These (who awake) shall be unto life everlasting, but those (who do not awake at that time) shall be unto shame and contempt everlasting.'" Dr. S. P. Tregelles confirms this interpretation. In other words, not only the living saved of Israel, but also the resurrected regenerate of Israel will enter into the blessings of the kingdom. Those who remain asleep will, of course, be judged at the great white throne.

One other great foe is dealt with at the Second Advent. "The dragon, that old serpent, which is the devil and Satan," is to be bound and incarcerated for a thousand years in a mysterious prison described as "the abyss" (Revelation 20:1-3). During the whole of the history of the human race this implacable foe has attempted to cause the downfall of man and to frustrate the purposes of God. For the whole of our Lord's glorious reign he will be unable to deceive the nations or to seduce them from God, to blind men's minds or to attack the godly. The evil tempter will be under restraint.

Thus sin will be dealt with and the sinner removed before the golden age of the millennium commences. Every foe will be crushed, and the mighty Son of God will be supremely victorious over all who have opposed Him or His people.

 # The Reign of Christ

"THE KINGDOM of God," says Professor F. F. Bruce, "is a basic and recurring theme in the Old Testament. The song of Moses, sung after the safe passage of the Red Sea, concludes with the words, 'Jehovah shall reign for ever and ever' (Exodus 15:18). The kingship of God is not only eternal but universal. 'Jehovah hath established His throne in the heavens; and His kingdom ruleth over all' (Psalm 103:19). On earth, His kingship was manifested particularly in the national life of Israel. . . . With the decline and fall of the Davidic dynasty, the expectation of a future and more permanent manifestation of the kingship of God emerged with increasing clarity and can be traced from the Old Testament prophets right on into our Lord's lifetime." If prophecy is to be fulfilled, there must be a literal kingdom established on earth and subject to the rule of God. Daniel 7:13, 14, for example, declares that the Son of man shall receive an everlasting dominion and a kingdom which shall not be destroyed and that all peoples shall serve Him. Daniel 2 also makes it clear that when the Gentile empires have run their course, a theocratic kingdom shall crush them and then rapidly expand to fill the earth.

The predicted kingdom is obviously to be identified with the future rule of Christ. In the course of the annunciation to Mary, the angel Gabriel declared of the promised Babe, "He shall be great, and shall be called the Son of the Highest: and the Lord God shall give unto Him the throne of his father David: and He shall rule over the house of Jacob for ever; and of His kingdom there shall be no end" (Luke 1: 32, 33). When three decades later our Lord commenced His ministry at Capernaum, it was with the statement, "the kingdom of heaven is at hand" (Matthew 4:17), and Matthew adds that He preached the gospel of the kingdom in all the synagogues in Galilee (Matthew 4:23). The Jews were, of course, familiar with their own prophets, and they patently realized the implication of Christ's words. His disciples fully anticipated the establishment of the kingdom during His lifetime, and even after His resurrection they asked Him, "Wilt Thou at this time restore again the kingdom to Israel?" and the Master had to tell them, "It is not for you to know the times or the seasons" (Acts 1: 6-8).

Although it is evident that both the Jews and the disciples interpreted our Lord's references to the kingdom as implying the establishment of a literal kingdom upon earth, it is often maintained that He never intended this and that His statements were susceptible to other interpretations. Pentecost says, "To some the kingdom of God is synonymous with the eternal state or heaven into which one comes after death, so that it has no relationship to the earth whatsoever. To others it is a non-material or 'spiritual' kingdom, in which God rules over the hearts of men, so that while it is related to the present age, it is unrelated to earth. To still others, the kingdom is purely earthly, without spiritual realities attached to it, so that it is a political and social structure to be achieved by the efforts of men and thus becomes the goal of the social and economic revolution to which men press. To others, with the same general concept, it has to do with a nationalistic movement on the part of Israel that will reconstitute that nation as an independent nation in the political realm. Then there are those who view the kingdom as synonymous with the visible organized Church, so that the church becomes the kingdom, both spiritual and political." There can, however, be only one conclusion in view of the specific statements of some of the Old Testament prophets, viz., that there is to be a literal earthly kingdom under a theocratic rule. Some of the predicted conditions of that age are of such a character that they cannot be interpreted logically in any other way than literally; attempts to spiritualize them and to apply them to the church or the church age produce obvious inconsistencies and anomalies. One writer says that the promise is of a kingdom, "as literal as the historical kingdom of Israel. All prophecy from first to last asserts and implies such literality; in such details as location, nature, rulers, citizens, and the nations involved; in the fact that it will destroy and supplant literal kingdoms; in its direct connection as a restoration and continuation of the historical and Davidic kingdom."

At our Lord's return to earth, judgment will be executed upon the guilty, and condemned sinners will be consigned to eternal punishment (Matthew 25:41). This is a necessary preliminary to the institution of the kingdom, for all causes of stumbling or offence and all who practise lawlessness must first be removed (Matthew 13:41). The world which rejected Christ at His first advent will acclaim Him as King of kings and Lord of lords at His second advent. Every ruler will acknowledge His suzerainty, and the whole universe will be brought into subjection to the Supreme Ruler, for He shall put down all rule, authority and power.

If the Old Testament covenants are to be fulfilled, Israel must be restored to the land which was pledged to Abraham, and the prophets reveal that they are to be Divinely gathered out of the nations of the world and brought from all parts of the earth to be reinstated in their own land (Isaiah 43:5-7; Jeremiah 12:15; Ezekiel 28:25, 26; Amos 9:14, 15; Zephaniah 3:20; Zechariah 10:10). An unregenerate people would only revert sooner or later to the sinful practices of earlier days, however, and God has consequently declared that He will cleanse Israel's race from their sins and put a new spirit within them and change their hearts or nature

(Jeremiah 31:33, 34; Ezekiel 11:19; 36:25, 26; Zechariah 13:1). A nation will be born in a day, and the apostle Paul foretells that "all Israel shall be saved" (Romans 11:26), so widespread will be the conversion of the people. What is envisaged is not, of course, the regeneration of every member of the nation; the apostle makes it quite plain, ". . . they are not all Israel, which are of Israel" (Romans 9:6). But Israel will again be God's chosen people, and the nation will be exalted above all others (Isaiah 49:22, 23; 60:14-16).

Blessing will not be restricted to Israel. Gentiles who are converted during the period after the rapture of the church (Revelation 7:9-14) will be preserved from condemnation at the judgment of the living nations (Matthew 25:34) and will enter into millennial bliss. Many of the Old Testament Scriptures foretell the blessing of Gentiles in that golden age (Isaiah 56:6, 7), and Zechariah declares that those left of the nations shall go up to Jerusalem each year to worship the King, the Lord of hosts, at the feast of tabernacles (Zechariah 14:16-19).

The Second Advent of Christ will evidently be accompanied by physical disturbances which have the widest effect on the topography of Palestine. John indicates that just prior to our Lord's coming to execute vengeance upon a guilty world, there will be a great earthquake, more terrible than any which has preceded it (Revelation 16:18), while Zechariah declares that at His coming and the attendant happenings, the people will flee as they "fled from before the earthquake in the days of Uzziah king of Judah" (Zechariah 14:5) — tacitly confirming the words of the later seer. Haggai reveals that in the day of jugment God will shake both heaven and earth (Haggai 2:6), and Isaiah declares that God will visit Jerusalem with thunder and earthquake (Isaiah 29:6). Scriptures might be multiplied, but it seems quite clear that at our Lord's return to earth there will be a seismic disturbance of an unprecedented character. Several of its effects are also disclosed in the Scriptures. Micah plainly states, ". . . in the last days . . . the mountain of the house of the Lord shall be established in the top of the mountains, and it shall be exalted above the hills. . . ." (Micah 4:1). This seems a sheer impossibility, but Isaiah predicts in detail the events preceding that state. Tremendous upheavals will apparently lift up valleys and level down mountains and hills, the crooked will be straightened and the rough places will be smoothed into plain (Isaiah 40:4, 5). The whole area has, of course, suffered from earthquakes in the past, but what is foretold is an earthquake of unparalleled effect.

Revelation 16:19 states, "And the great city was divided into three parts, and the cities of the nations fell. . . .," and Zechariah further reveals that at Messiah's descent ". . . His feet shall stand in that day upon the mount of Olives . . . and the mount of Olives shall cleave in the midst thereof toward the east and toward the west, and there shall be a very great valley; and half of the mountain shall remove toward the north, and half of it toward the south" (Zechariah 14:4). A glance at the map will show at once the effect of such a remarkable cleavage. In conjunction with the sudden submergence of some land and the elevation of other as described by Isaiah, these violent changes will almost inevitably result in the country's suffering from floods and possibly other catastrophes. The Jordan valley, which is the deepest depression in the world, runs from north to south and finishes in the Dead Sea, but the sudden introduction of a new valley from east to west might well affect the course of the river. The great rift will completely alter the contour of the country, and the upheaval will thrust up the mountain on which the temple is built, so that it will be higher than all the surrouding hills. It is clear from Zechariah 14:10 that the area from Geba, six miles north of Jerusalem, to Rimmon, thirty miles south of the city, will be transformed into a plain dominated by the Holy City at its new exalted height.

Dr. Mabie's description is well worth quoting *in extenso*: "This earthquake will not only change the whole topography of Palestine, but it will cut in two the mountain backbone of that land, right through the Mount of Olives. By it at one stroke, east and west, the land will divide, and a great ship canal be formed from the Mediterranean Sea to the Jordan valley and the Dead Sea. The waters of the great sea, rushing down through that earthquake chasm, with a fall about eight times the height of Niagara — or an average of about 22 feet to the mile — would fill the Jordan valley to the Sea of Galilee and above. To the southward the waters would sweep down to the Gulf of Aqaba and the Red Sea. So, if the Jordan valley should remain at about its present level, it would form the bed of a great and deep inland sea, approaching to the very suburbs of Jerusalem. So the city of the great king would become the seaport of the world — the business emporium of the nations." This is no idle fantasy, for Zechariah plainly states that in that day, "living waters shall go out from Jerusalem; half of them toward the former sea (i.e., the eastern Dead Sea) and half of them toward the hinder sea" (i.e., the western or Mediterranean Sea) (Zechariah 14:8) In other words, Jerusalem will stand on a great canal uniting the Mediterranean and Dead Seas, and it will presumably be practicable for navigation to use the channel to reach the city and the interior of the country. The commercial potentialities are patent. No warlike vessel will pass there (Isaiah 33:21).

These are not the only new features of the land. In Ezekiel's vision of the millennial temple, there is no trace of the brazen laver of the Old Testament tabernacle or of the brazen sea of Solomon's temple. Instead, a river gushes up in the holy of holies and flows under the door of the temple, through the temple court and into the Dead Sea, bringing a new life into the salt lake, so that fishermen in the future will gather there to find fish like those of the Mediterranean. In *The Prophetic Outlook Today*, E. P. Cachemaille suggests that the summit of the mountain on which the millennial temple is built will be so high as to be in perpetual snow, and that the melting snows will supply the great river which flows out of the sanctuary to water the thirsty land.

The physical changes in the land adequately account for the prophet's description of the construction of the temple, the site of the holy oblation, the prince's portion and the city's possession (Ezekiel 45:1-8; 48:8-21). Cachemaille's description of this area is well worth quoting. "By the border of Judah there is to be a holy portion of land set apart as an oblation to the Lord. It is a square of twenty-five thousand reeds or forty-four miles to the side, taking the reed as nine feet, four inches. It is divided into three strips from east to west thus: one strip of 10,000 reeds broad for the priests, the same for the Levites, and one of 5,000 for the city. Those for the priests and Levites would be each about nineteen miles wide; that for the city about ten miles. The priests' portion is for the sanctuary and their dwellings, so for the Levites and their dwellings. In the middle of the priests' portion is the very high mountain, on the southern slope of which is the sanctuary, the Lord's house looking like a city in size and appearance, and facing towards the east. It is a temple and its courts, surrounded by massive walls forming three terraces: the outer court, the inner court, and the temple itself. The enclosure is about three quarters of a mile square. The area assigned for the city is 25,000 reeds long by 5,000 wide, for common use of the city, for dwellings and for suburbs. In the midst stands the city, a square of 4,500 reeds — about eight miles — with suburbs on the four sides 250 reeds wide. On each side are three gates, bearing the names of the twelve tribes. This leaves a space of 10,000 reeds to the east and the same to the west, to be cultivated as market gardens for food for the citizens. On either side of the holy oblation, east and west, between the parallels of Judah and Benjamin, the remainder of the land not occupied by the holy oblations is to be the possession of the prince."

Considerable difficulty is felt by many commentators regarding the Biblical references to a sacrificial system in connection with the millennial temple. Ezekiel discloses that burnt offerings, sin offerings, trespass offerings, meal offerings and peace offerings, will again be presented (Ezekiel 40:39; 42:13; 43:18, 27). This seems completely incompatible with the finality of Calvary's work, and many have suggested that the reinstitution of a sacrificial system and the restoration of a priesthood cannot have been intended to be interpreted literally. The only feasible explanation is that the millennial sacrifices are not expiatory but memorial in character. As Dr. Skevington Wood says, "when the church has been raptured and God brings Israel once more into blessing, a new dispensation will have dawned and with it a further revelation of God's purposes. The temple will then be rebuilt, the priesthood reintroduced and the sacrifices renewed, so that in the light of Christ, the true Messiah, and the one sacrifice for sin, these may accomplish what all along had been their ultimate purpose. Just as the offerings on the altar of Solomon's temple pointed forward to Calvary, so these will look back. They will commemorate an accomplished redemption and at the same time express the deepest intention of the law."

The blessings of the millennium will be manifold. As one writer says, "Though the principal effects of the reign of Christ will be manifested in righteous government and in the spiritual realm, the rule of Christ will have extensive impact on the economic and social aspects of life on the earth." Wars will cease, and peace will prevail universally. Micah declares that the nations, ". . . shall beat their swords into ploughshares, and their spears into pruning-hooks: nation shall not lift up a sword against nation, neither shall they learn war any more" (Micah 4:3). The Messianic rule will be in perfect justice and equity, and righteousness will pervade the scene (Isaiah 9:7; 11:5; 32:16, 17). Holiness will characterize the people of God, and their land, city and possessions will be sanctified to God (Zechariah 14:20, 21). In such conditions, crime will be reduced to a minimum, but sin will be punished by death (Isaiah 65:20).

During our Lord's earthly life He brought healing to the sick and sight to the blind. Under His beneficent rule in the golden age, the blind will receive their sight; the dumb will be enabled to speak and the deaf to hear; the cripple will throw away his crutches and leap for joy; those suffering from other physical disabilities will be healed; and sickness will be cured (Isaiah 29:18; 33:24; 35:5, 6). The grief of the brokenhearted will be converted into joy, and praise will be substituted for heaviness (Isaiah 61:1-3). Possibly as a natural corollary to the banishment of sickness, longevity will characterize the race: a person who dies at one hundred will be deemed a little child (Isaiah 65:20). The depopulation caused by judgment prior to the establishment of the kingdom will be compensated by a greatly increased birthrate throughout the world (Ezekiel 47:22), and the streets of Jerusalem will echo with the happy shouting of the crowds of playing children (Zechariah 8:5).

Adam's sin invoked a Divine curse upon creation (Genesis 3:17-19), and nature has suffered ever since. But in that day the curse will be lifted; thorn and briar will disappear, and the desert will blossom as the rose (Isaiah 35:1, 2). An abundance of rain will result in increased productivity of the land; food will be plentiful and flocks and herds will increase (Isaiah 30:23, 24). The picture painted is one of prosperity and fruitfulness, every man possessing his own dwelling and field and sitting under his own vine and fig tree (Micah 4:4). So bountiful will be the blessing that the prophet declares, ". . . the ploughman shall overtake the reaper, and the treader of grapes him that soweth seed. . ." (Amos 9:13); the tremendously increased fertility thus speeding up the rate of growth and increasing the number of harvests, the reaping being followed immediately by a fresh sowing. The very animal creation will lose its venom and ferocity. "The wolf also shall dwell with the lamb, and the leopard shall lie down with the kid; and the calf and the young lion and the fatling together; and a little child shall lead them. And the cow and the bear shall feed; their young ones shall lie down together: and the lion shall eat straw like the ox. And the sucking child shall play on the hole of the asp, and the weaned child shall put his hand on the cockatrice' den. They shall not hurt nor destroy in all my holy mountain. . ." (Isaiah 11:6-9; 65:25).

Our Lord is to be supreme potentate, and every ruler will be subject to Him. God will bestow upon Him the nations as an inheritance and the uttermost part of the earth as a possession (Psalm 2:8; Zechariah 14:9). As His vice-regent in Israel, a prince of the house of David will sit upon the throne — a man who has sons, who must bring sin offerings for himself and his people, and who must avail himself of the ministry of the priesthood (Ezekiel 45:22; 46:2). Christ is not, of course, identified with the prince but with the shekinah glory which fills the temple (Ezekiel 43:1-5).

Six times in Revelation 20 is the period during which Christ is to rule described as a thousand years, but in no other Scripture is the duration stated. In consequence, it has often been suggested that the millennium is not intended as an actual period of time but rather as a picture of the spiritual blessing enjoyed by the church. As already indicated, however, a careful study of the Old Testament prophets leads inevitably to the conclusion that a glorious reign upon earth has been pledged. Whether a thousand years is intended to convey the idea of a period of ten centuries, or whether the term is used as a symbol of a very long period, may be a matter on which dogmatism is inadvisable, but there is no doubt that a complete age of considerable duration is envisaged.

But the reign of Christ is not limited to earth. Philippians 2:9-11 makes it clear that every celestial, terrestrial and infernal creature shall bow in obeisance to Him and humbly acknowledge His lordship. In his letter to the Ephesian church, the apostle Paul states that God has purposed, "that, in the dispensation of the fullness of times, He might gather together in one all things in Christ, both which are in the heavens, and which are on earth" (Ephesians 1:10). The whole universe is to be bound together under the supreme rule of our Sovereign Lord. If this tiny planet is to own His sway, it is but a trivial part of the galactic Milky Way with its 100,000 millions of stars and planets; the Milky Way itself is only a small galaxy among the trillions of galaxies which stretch out into the far distances of space; and our Lord Jesus Christ is to be the supreme Ruler over them all. In that glorious day there will be no sphere in which He is not heralded as King; there will be no tongue which will not acclaim Him as Lord; there will be no knee which shall not bow in homage to Him. He will reign through all the vast extent of God's creatorial work.

 # The Final Revolt

DURING THE thousand years of Christ's reign over the earth, the nations will be compelled to recognize His power and might, for He is to rule with a rod of iron and to dash to pieces any who dare lift themselves up against Him (Psalm 2:8, 9). Discontent and disloyalty will be driven underground by fear, and malcontents will render feigned obedience to Him (Psalm 66:3, margin). Any sign of resistance will be punished immediately by death. G. F. Trench suggests that the age, "is one of constant, discriminating judgment, detecting, convicting and punishing by death all those in whose lives sin breaks out in overt acts." Nevertheless, Divine blessing will cover the earth, and prosperity will be the universal experience.

Despite all the tokens of God's goodness during the long millennial age, there will be masses of people who have never turned to God and who remain unrepentant still. Conscious of the evil of their own hearts, such will shrink from the holiness of God's earthly center and will gravitate to areas as far away as possible from Jerusalem — "the four corners of the earth." There they will share their common antipathy to the Messianic rule and evidence their incorrigible hostility to the King and their antagonism to righteousness and holiness. As the centuries elapse, there will doubtless be large accretions to the ranks of the malcontents until, at the close of the dispensation, vast numbers will be in a state of incipient revolt against the rule of Christ and His people. Human nature is incurably corrupt, and every test — even in the most favorable conditions of the millennium — serves but to demonstrate man's complete inability apart from Divine help to live in a manner glorifying to God.

At the commencement of the millennium, the devil will be held prisoner in what the Apocalypse terms "the bottomless pit" (Revelation 20:2). For a thousand years his unceasing activity will be halted and mankind freed from his malevolent influence, but at the close of the age he will be released for "a little season" (Revelation 20:3). With unabated hatred of God, he will issue forth, "to deceive the nations which are in the four corners of the earth." The precise procedure adopted or the exact nature of his deception is not stated, but it is probable that the Satanic appeal to the nations will be to establish their own government and to overthrow that of the Messiah. Galled by the superior position of Israel and their own enforced subordination to a nation so long despised, they will readily respond to the appeal and will gather together to battle. The Revelation discloses that the rebellious hosts will be as numberless as the sands of the sea. During the millennium all nations will be required to go up to Jerusalem at the feast of tabernacles (Zechariah 14:16); this may, of course, imply delegations from each nation rather than the total population of each country. The majority of Jews will naturally assemble at the temple in Jerusalem for the feast. The obligation on the nations to be represented at Jerusalem for the feast at that period will only emphasize the Gentiles' subjection to Israel and consequently exacerbate still further their bitter resentment. Evidently the opportunity will be seized for a large number to make their way to the city without exciting suspicion.

With their Trojan horse within the gates, the great army gathered by the devil will audaciously attack the city, clearly with the intention of massacring the followers of Christ and possibly of destroying the King as well. Heaven's answer will be swift and inexorable, for before a sword is unsheathed or a weapon used, the fire of God will fall upon the rebels and consume them (Revelation 20:9). The devil, the age-long deceiver of mankind, having now been finally defeated, will be cast forever into the "lake of fire," there to join the western emperor and the Jewish ruler who were consigned to that place of suffering a thousand years earlier. This is final and conclusive. The ill-fated rebellion, after such a long period of bliss and prosperity, is a sad commentary on human nature, unaffected and unchanged by the King's beneficence. Trench writes, "The millennium, instead of being the consummation, the final and perfect state of the world's history, and the plenary fulfillment of the prophecies of the Kingly glory of Christ is, in fact, the last of a long series of Divine tests by which man in the flesh has been proved by God. It is also the severest test of all, because it is a condition of privilege higher than man ever enjoyed before."

Well over 4,000 years ago, the extent of man's sin and disregard of every moral and spiritual standard provoked judgment on the race and the earth which they inhabited. With the exception of one family of eight persons, every human being perished in the Flood, and Peter declared that the world "being overflowed with water, perished." Because of the sin of a later day, judgment will again fall upon the earth, and since the heavens too are defiled (Job 15:15), they also will suffer at the hand of God. Destruction on this occasion will not be by water but by fire; "the heavens and the earth," says the apostle, "are reserved unto fire against the day of judgment." The destruction of that future day is to be devastatingly complete. It will come, unexpected as a thief. On that day the heavens will disappear with a great rushing sound, the elements will disintegrate in flames and the earth with all that is in it, will be laid bare. Since the whole universe is to break up in this way, that day will set the heavens ablaze until they fall apart, and will melt the elements in flames (II Peter 3:10-12). Centuries earlier

Isaiah had predicted, "the heavens shall vanish away like smoke, and the earth shall wax old like a garment, and they that dwell therein shall die in like manner" (Isaiah 51:6). Joel refers to that period as one in which there will be "blood and fire and pillars of smoke" (Joel 2:30). The ultimate dissolution of the world is clearly inevitable. "Heaven and earth shall pass away," said the Master (Matthew 24:35). The Psalmist also predicted that the heavens and the earth should perish (Psalm 102:25-26), and the Apocalypse declares that from the face of the Almighty, ". . . the earth and the heaven fled away; and there was found no place for them" (Revelation 20:11). The words used by Joel and Peter centuries ago could well have been a description of an atomic explosion on a gigantic scale; the great rushing sound as the huge pillar of smoke ascends and breaks out into a tremendous mushroom formation, the blazing fire and blood-red cloud, the fission of atoms and disintegration of the elements — the whole picture of nuclear horrors was painted in vivid but restrained language by the Biblical writers centuries ago. The earth and its ethereal garments are to be completely dissolved and the whole of their matter converted into heat, light and energy. A sin-stained earth can find no place in eternity.

Dispensations having come to an end, the final and irrevocable decision must be taken regarding the fate of the dead. People living at the Second Advent of Christ will be dealt with at the judgment of the nations prior to the institution of the millennial kingdom, and the condemned will pass into eternal punishment (Matthew 25:31-46). The Christian dead will have been raised at an earlier date (I Thessalonians 4:16), and the martyrs of the tribulation period will be raised at the beginning of the millennium to reign with Christ for a thousand years (Revelation 20:4). But the rest of the dead, i.e., all the unregenerate, will remain in the grave until the close of the millennium; after the final revolt and possibly coincidentally with the dissolution of the earth, they are to be raised for judgment.

John saw, poised in space without pillar or support, a great white throne, its purity indicative of the holiness and perfect righteousness of the invisible Occupant and the justice of His decisions, and its greatness indicating not only His infinite majesty and authority, but the finality of the sentence pronounced from that throne. There could be no appeal from that court. All the impenitent — dead spiritually and in most cases physically — are to be summoned for the last judgment; great and small must stand before the Judge. A century ago the description of a final assize conducted in space seemed unrealistic, but no one today would question the practicability.

In absolute equity, the records of human life will be unrolled — "the books were opened" — and each individual dealt with on the basis of his deeds. No oral evidence will be required as in human courts; from the recesses of the individual's own memory the whole story will be revealed and flashed instantaneously before his mind. Each person will be judged according to his works, plainly implying that there are to be degrees of punishment and that the judgment is to be a fitting requital. Lest any question could be raised, the seer declares that the book of life will also be opened. The final condemnation must be the absence of the name from that record. The consciousness of their true condition will be borne in upon those who appear before the throne, and in the sudden realization of their guilt and uncleanness, their only desire will be to remove themselves as far as possible from the holiness and purity of that awful throne. They will acquiesce completely with the sentence of eternal banishment from God and the terrible consignment to the second death, the lake of fire (Revelation 20:11-15). The justice of the sentence will be so obvious that no question can possibly arise. Sin must be punished. Whatever may be implied by a "lake of fire" is not clear, but if the symbol is dreadful, how awful must be the reality. Whatever may be the character of that place of eternal punishment, it is clear that it will be one of permanent and unrelieved suffering.

Judgment concluded, the apostle John saw in a vision, ". . . a new heaven and a new earth: for the first heaven and the first earth were passed away, and there was no more sea" (Revelation 21:1). The apostle stood on the threshold of the eternal day, and a new heaven and a new earth appeared before his eyes. "The new heaven is for the raised and changed saints," says Scott, and, "the new earth is to form the habitation of those who, during the millennial reign, were alive on earth — those companies described in Revelation 7 and 14" — but it is by no means clear that the inhabitants of the new-made world will be restricted to the believers of the millennial era.

Three quarters of the globe is at present occupied by the sea. In the new earth, there is to be no sea; the restless oceans will retreat to provide a world which is completely habitable. The troubled sea is a frequent figure in Scripture of the restless masses of mankind, and its destructive and separative character is remarkable symbolic of the effects of sin upon the human race. "But the wicked are like the troubled sea, when it cannot rest, whose waters cast up mire and dirt" (Isaiah 57:20).

I Corinthians 15:24-28 discloses that when the Lord Jesus Christ has, "put down all rule and all authority and power," and has "put all enemies under His feet," He will deliver up the kingdom to God the Father. His reign as Mediatorial King will come to an end when the mediatorial kingdom is incorporated in the eternal kingdom. It is usually suggested that Christ will thereupon cease to reign over the earth or any part of it, but there is no Biblical reference to His alleged abdication, and Revelation 22:3 specifically refers to "the throne of God and of the Lamb." Peters says, "Jesus Christ still reigns, either as God, the humanity being subordinate, or as God-Man." The end of the mediatorial kingdom is followed by the commencement of the timeless and unending period of the eternal state. God's tabernacle or center of administration in the form of a beautiful city will descend from heaven, and God will dwell among the inhabitants of the earth and will be their God. In that day death will be banished and grief, crying and distress will be abolished. Corruption and mortality will find no place in the new economy. The new earth will be a scene of beauty and a sphere of spiritual blessing, but the details recorded are limited and do not fully indicate the incomparable bliss of eternity.

 # The Divine Plan

THE PRECEDING chapters cover many of the events in the Divine program, but it may help to a clearer understanding if an outline is given of the order of prophetic events. The greater part of what follows is taken from the author's book, *Prophecy's Last Word*. It also recapitulates some of the details already mentioned.

All prophecy is, of course, centered in the Person of the Lord Jesus Christ and revolves about Him. He is the Hope of the church and the Desire of Israel; He is the Redeemer for whom creation groans and the Deliverer for whom the nations wait; He is the coming One who is yet to set all things in order.

When David was settled upon the throne of Israel, Jehovah entered into a covenant with him to establish his house and his kingdom for ever (II Samuel 7). The Davidic covenant has not yet been completely fulfilled but has never been abrogated: in a future day the Divine purpose will be realized. When our Lord descends to earth, all promises will find their satisfaction in Him, and the long-expected kingdom will at last be set up.

On the death of Solomon, the kingdom was divided into the two kingdoms of Israel and Judah, the former crowning Jeroboam as king and the latter retaining their loyalty to Rehoboam, Solomon's son. In 721 B.C., the sins of Israel resulted in the ten tribes being carried away captive into Assyria (II Kings 17). Judah, however, proved no less guilty, and in 598 B.C., Nebuchadnezzar carried into Mesopotamia

Jehoiachin and the chief people of Judah (II Kings 24). As a result of Zedekiah's rebellion nine years later, Jerusalem was burnt and the majority of the people carried away. God thus removed the testimony of Israel as a whole, and the sword of government passed into the hands of the Gentiles in the person of Nebuchadnezzar, and to this heathen monarch God committed the potential dominion of the world (Daniel 2:37, 38).

It was revealed to Nebuchadnezzar (in the vision of the great image of four metals) that, from the rise of the Babylonian monarchy to the end of the age, the sword of world government would pass through the hands of four great empires, following upon which was to come the establishment of "the kingdom of the heavens." The first of these empires is stated to be the Babylonian, and history makes it clear that the three successive empires were those of Medo-Persia, Greece and Rome. The last of these, however, disappeared as an empire before reaching the final condition foretold in Daniel 2 and 7. If God's Word is to be fulfilled, the Roman empire must still have a future, and we may reasonably anticipate a re-emergence into prominence of this fourth great power.

In a further revelation to Daniel (Daniel 9) it was disclosed that "seventy weeks" were decreed upon his people (i.e., the Jews). It is clear that the "weeks" (lit., "sevens") were weeks of years and that each week is the equivalent of seven years. The period of these prophetic weeks commenced with the going forth of the commandment to restore and to build Jerusalem (Daniel 9:25), which, as Nehemiah 2 makes evident, was in the twentieth year of Artaxerxes or 445 B.C.

The seventy weeks were divided into three sections, viz:

(1) Seven weeks or forty-nine years were to be spent in the rebuilding of the city.

(2) Sixty-two weeks or four hundred thirty-four years were to elapse from then until Messiah the Prince.

(3) After the cutting off of Messiah, the last week of seven years was to run its course.

The first era of forty-nine years was exactly fulfilled. After the sixty-ninth week (actually during the same *literal* week), Messiah was cut off as foretold by the prophecy. The seventieth week of Daniel 9, which had yet to run its course, must either have followed immediately upon the sixty-nine weeks or have been separated from them by some intervening period. Since the first sixty-nine "weeks" were weeks of years, it follows that the final week must be the equivalent of seven years also.

The events which were to occur during that final period of seven years are carefully detailed in Daniel 9:27, and it is quite clear from history that these events have not yet taken place. It is a legitimate assumption, therefore, that a break occurred in the continuity of the "weeks", and that the whole of the present dispensation falls as a parenthesis between the end of the sixty-ninth week and the beginning of the seventieth week. (This is dealt with in detail in the author's book, *The Climax of the Ages*.)

When the Jews rejected their Messiah, God suspended His dealings with an earthly people and commenced to call out a heavenly people — a church composed of all those born of, and indwelt by, the Holy Spirit. Until Calvary God had dealt with individuals and peoples as Israelites or Gentiles, but that difference has been abolished during the present age (Ephesians 2:14), and He now deals with individuals as saints or sinners, as members or non-members of the church of God. This church was a mystery hidden in previous ages until the time came for its revelation (Ephesians 3:5, 6). Hence there is no mention of the church or the church-age in the Old Testament. When the church age comes to a close, judgment and blessing will again be dispensed on a national basis, and Israel will occupy her former position of the favored nation, and Daniel's postponed seventieth week will at last commence. The length of the present dispensation is not stated in Scripture, but its history, so far as the church is concerned, is possibly delineated in Revelation 2 and 3. So far as Christendom generally is concerned, there may also be a foreshadowing in the parables of Matthew 13.

The present age, which commenced with the descent of the Holy Spirit (Acts 2), is peculiarly the age of the Spirit and will end at His removal from the world (II Thessalonians 2:7). This event will apparently coincide with the rapture of the true church.

The glorious future which awaits the church is to be united to her risen Head, and every true believer accordingly waits for the second advent of Christ. The date of that coming has been withheld, but all events of the present day indicate the imminence of the event. I Thessalonians 4:15-17 reveals that the Lord Jesus Christ will personally descend into the air, the dead in Christ be raised and, together with the living saints, be caught up to meet Him in the air, never again to be separated from Him or from each other. Every member of the church will be caught away and not a single one be left behind. I Corinthians 15:51-53 unfolds the additional facts that the dead will be raised incorruptible and that the living will be changed from mortality to immortality. The theory of a partial rapture is, of course, without Scriptural support (see e.g., I Thessalonians 5:10).

After the rapture there will appropriately follow the individual examination of believers at the *bema* or judgment seat of Christ (II Corinthians 5:10) where each will receive a reward or suffer loss according to the deeds done in the body. When the saints have been arrayed in the fine linen of their righteous deeds, the church will be united to the

Lamb in marriage (Revelation 19) prior to her manifestation with Him in glory (II Thessalonians 1:10, etc.).

The full display of Satan's activities on earth is at present hindered by the two influences described in II Thessalonians 2 as "what withholdeth" (v. 6) and "He who now letteth" (v. 7), that is, respectively, the church and the Holy Spirit who indwells it. Both these restraining influences will be removed at the rapture, and Satan will then be at liberty to produce his masterpiece, "the man of sin."

Prophecy indicates that at the end of the present dispensation Israel will be found in her own land once more, the old Mosaic ritual restored and that a Jewish king will reign at Jerusalem (Daniel 11:36-39, etc.). This king will subsequently be manifested as "the false prophet" of Revelation 16:13, etc.

The great image of Nebuchadnezzar's vision ended in ten toes, and the fourth beast of Daniel's vision possessed ten horns (Daniel 2 and 7), indicating a phase of Roman history which has not yet been seen. Other prophecies imply that the Roman empire is one day to be revived in the new form of a confederacy of ten kingdoms (Revelation 13:1-3) with a great emperor at the head. This monarch (the Beast of Revelation) will commence his career with the subjugation of three kingdoms after which seven others will surrender their power to him (Daniel 7:24; Revelation 17:13). To this man Satan will give the supreme power or world authority which he offered to our Lord (Revelation 13:4).

Among other characters in God's prophetic program are the kings of the north and sourth. Daniel 11 describes the wars, intrigues and alliances of the kingdoms of Syria and Egypt down to the day of Antiochus Epiphanes, but from verse 40 the future activities of these two powers are brought under review. The king of the south is, of course, Egypt. The king of the north is apparently a ruler in Asia Minor who is under the protection of the great northern confederacy of Joel 2, the Assyrian of Isaiah 10.

After the removal of the church, its travesty will be produced in the Great Whore who sits upon many waters (Revelation 17), i.e., who rules ecclesiastically over multitudes and nations with a power surpassing even papal hopes and expectations. This religious Babylon will evidently cover the sects and denominations of Christendom and possibly other religious systems as well — the one world church for which men have so long striven. When the process of welding the nations together by the power of religion has been completed, the great empire will destroy the whole system and confiscate its wealth (Revelation 17:16).

The Jewish State, because of its geographical position, will obviously be under constant threat from both the north and the south, and in order to preserve the little country as a buffer state and to prevent other powers from taking over the Middle East, the western ruler will enter into a seven year agreement with the Jews, guaranteeing them protection from their foes (Daniel 9:27). The strength of the northern power will be so great, however, that the western powers will be unable to prevent the inevitable invasion, and the northern forces will sweep down into the land, laying Jerusalem in heaps and shedding blood like water (Psalm 74, 79, 83, etc.).

Halfway through the seventieth week of Daniel 9 (with which the seven years of the treaty synchronize), the Beast will suddenly put a stop to the revived Mosaic ritual and worship and force idolatry upon the Jews and upon the ten kingdoms over which he reigns. An image of himself will be set up in the temple, and divine honours claimed for the image and for the one whom it represents (Daniel 9:27; II Thessalonians 2:4). This event marks the commencement of the terrible period known in Scripture as the time of Jacob's trouble or the great tribulation. The subsequent three and one-half years represent the same period as the

1260 days of Revelation 12:6; the time, times and half a time of Revelation 12:14; and the forty-two months of Revelation 13:5. During those few years, Palestine will be a scene of warfare and terrible slaughter, the horror of which is not exaggerated by the language of the Psalms that allude to it. Throughout the western empire, as well as in Palestine, all will be compelled on pain of death to worship the Beast and to receive his mark in their right hand or in their forehead, no trading being allowed without the mark, the name, or the number of the name (Revelation 13:16, 17). The great tribulation will also be characterized by God's judgment of His guilty people and by the outpouring upon earth of the Divine judgments of the seals, trumpets and vials of Revelation 6 to 16 with the ultimate result of universal chaos and the complete disruption of civil and political society. Even during this period, God will have His witnesses (Revelation 11) and many will be converted (Revelation 7 and 14).

In the last days Satan will gather together the western hosts in the plain of Megiddo to besiege the godly remnant in Jerusalem (Zechariah 13; Revelation 16:16, etc.). Suddenly Christ will come with all His saints to make war upon His enemies. The mount of Olives will cleave in the midst at His descent (Zechariah 14). The mighty Conqueror will ride forth with the sword and give their flesh to the fowls to eat (Revelation 19:11-31). The Beast and the false prophet will be cast into the lake of fire (Revelation 19:20), the first inhabitants of that awful place.

At that time, the king of the north will be conducting a war in the south against Egypt (Daniel 11:42, 43), but the tidings of Christ's return will come to him from the northeast, i.e., Palestine, and he will promptly return in fury to destroy and make war on the Lamb (Daniel 11:44). Seeking to fight the Omnipotent, he and his armies will perish on the mountains of Israel with none to help. Satan, the author of evil, will be taken, bound and then cast into the bottomless pit, there to remain for a thousand years (Revelation 20: 1-3).

Apparently only a part of Israel will return to Palestine prior to our Lord's return to earth. After the battle of Armageddon, the remainder of Israel will be gathered out of the nations of the world (Isaiah 11:11, 12; Ezekiel 20 and 34) and brought into the wilderness (Hosea 12:13), where Jehovah will plead with them and after passing them under the rod will eventually restore them to the land (Amos 9:15; Zephaniah 3:14-20). The two kingdoms of Israel and Judah, after centuries of division, will be reunited under one head (Ezekiel 37) and will rejoice in a national conversion (Jeremiah 31, 33, 34; Ezekiel 36:24-31; Zechariah 13:1).

His enemies overthrown, the Lord Jesus Christ will proceed to set up His earthly tribunal, and the living nations will be summoned before Him to judgment (Matthew 25). The result will be a tremendous depopulation of the earth which will, to some extent, be repaired by means of longevity of life and human fruitfulness during the millennium.

When all disorder has been removed and judgment has been carried out, the kingdom of God will at last be established on earth. The Davidic covenant will find its complete fulfillment with Israel as the head of the nations (Micah 4:8) and the center of blessing, a prince of the house of David sitting on the throne of Jerusalem, and the kingdom established for the remainder of earthly history until the ages of time give place to the eternal state. The twelve tribes of Israel will spread in parallel bands across the country from the Euphrates to the Mediterranean. The glory of Jehovah will again fill the temple, and Levitical priests will once more minister before Him. For a thousand years Christ will reign in righteousness and equity (Jeremiah 23:5, 6; Zechariah 6:12, 13); peace and joy will pervade the scene. The millennium is the period of the "restitution of all things" — an age in which, ". . . the eyes of the blind shall be opened, and the ears of the deaf be unstopped. Then shall the lame man leap as an hart, and the tongue of the dumb sing. . ." (Isaiah 35:5). In that day all creation will be at peace, and, "The wolf and the lamb shall feed together, and the lion shall eat straw like the bullock. . ." (Isaiah 65:25). The prophets are full of the rest, tranquility and happiness of that age.

During the millennium, there will be universal submission to Christ, and He will be outwardly acknowledged as supreme Lord. Since the human heart is ever sinful, in many cases the subjection will be only a feigned obedience, and lip-service will hide inward opposition and enmity. At the close of that glorious dispensation, however, the true character of man will be evidenced. Satan will be loosed from his bondage for a little season and will go forth to deceive the nations, gathering them together against the city of Jerusalem in a final desperate effort to overthrow the king and the kingdom, but fire will come down from God out of heaven and destroy the rebellious hosts (Revelation 20). Satan will be cast for ever into the lake of fire, never again to issue forth on his evil missions. Heaven and earth removed, "the dead, small and great," will stand before the great white throne to be judged according to the things written in the books, and all those whose names are not found written in the book of life will be cast into the lake of fire (Revelation 20:15). Death and Hades, neither of which will then be any longer required, will also find their end in the lake of fire (Revelation 20:14).

II Peter 3 reveals that heaven and earth are to be purged with fire and that God will then bring into existence, "new heavens and a new earth, wherein dwelleth righteousness" (II Peter 3:10-13). Ages and dispensations will no longer have any part in Divine dealings, but all will give place to the eternal state in which everything is confirmed and consolidated. The abolition of the sea from the world (Revelation 21:1) will give an enormously larger scope for the earth-dwellers, who will presumably be the people converted during the millennium. The holy city, New Jerusalem, will descend from heaven as a bride adorned for her husband, and God will dwell with men, removing sorrow, sin and sickness. Everything on earth and in heaven will be perfect and holy, and God will be all and in all.

ACKNOWLEDGMENTS

We acknowledge with appreciation permission from the following for use of their material:

Abingdon Press, Nashville, for quotation from J. A. T. Robertson's book, *Jesus and His Coming,* © 1958.

Dallas Theological Seminary, Dallas, for material used from Lewis Sperry Chafer's, *Major Bible Themes,* © 1953.

Dunham Publishing Company, Grand Rapids, for material from *Things to Come,* by J. Dwight Pentecost, © 1958. Also, *The Millennial Kingdom,* by John F. Walvoord, © Revised 1963.

Wm. B. Eerdmans Publishing Co., Grand Rapids, for material quoted from, *The Second Coming of Christ,* by Louis Berkhof © 1953; also, from *The Gospel of the Kingdom,* by George E. Ladd, © 1959.

Loizeaux Brothers, Inc., Neptune, New Jersey, for a quotation from H. C. Thiessen's *Will the Church Pass Through the Tribulation?* © 1941.

Presbyterian & Reformed Publishing Co., Nutley, New Jersey, for material quoted from Oswald T. Allis, *Prophecy and the Church,* © 1945.

Charles Scribner's Sons, New York, for material quoted from *The Parables of the Kingdom,* by C. H. Dodd, © 1961.

The Strombeck Agency, Moline, Illinois, for material from the book, *First the Rapture,* by J. F. Strombeck, © 1950.

Every effort has been made to locate the source of all quotations used in the text of this book. However, this was not possible in all instances.

Bibliography

Alderman, P. R., *The Unfolding Of The Ages*. New York: Loizeaux Brothers, n.d.

Allis, Oswald T., *Prophecy And The Church*. Philadelphia: Presbyterian & Reformed Publishing Co., 1945.

Anderson, Sir Robert, *Daniel In The Critics' Den*. London: James Nisbet & Co., 1909.

————————————, *Human Destiny*. Glasgow: Pickering and Inglis, 1913.

————————————, *The Coming Prince*. Grand Rapids: Kregel Publications, 1967 (Reprint).

Anstey, M., *The Romance of Bible Chronology*. London: Marshall Brothers, 1913.

Atkinson, B. F. C., *The War With Satan*. London: Protestant Publishing Co., n.d.

Bass, Clarence E., *Backgrounds To Dispensationalism*. Grand Rapids: Wm. B. Eerdmans Publishing Co., 1960.

Beasley-Murray, G. R., *Jesus And The Future*. New York: Macmillan, 1954.

Beckwith, G., *God's Prophetic Plan Through The Ages*. Grand Rapids: Zondervan Publishing Co., 1942.

Berkhof, Louis, *The Kingdom of God*. Grand Rapids: Wm. B. Eerdmans Publishing Co., 1951.

————————————, *The Second Coming Of Christ*. Grand Rapids: Wm. B. Eerdmans Publishing Co., 1953.

Blackstone, Wm. E., *Jesus Is Coming*. Chicago: Fleming H. Revell, 1925.

Bradbury, J. W. (Editor), *Hastening The Day Of God*. Wheaton, Illinois: Van Kampen Press, 1953.

Bright, John, *The Kingdom Of God*. Nashville, Tennessee: Abingdon Press, 1953.

Brookes, J. H., *Maranatha*. New York: Fleming H. Revell, 1889.

Brown, C. E., *The Reign Of Christ*. Anderson, Indiana: Gospel Trumpet Co., 1948.

Burgh, W,. *Lectures On The Second Advent Of Our Lord Jesus Christ*. Dublin: P. M. Tims, 1832.

Campbell, Roderick, *Israel And The New Covenant*. Philadelphia: Presbyterian And Reformed Publishing Co., 1954.

Cameron, R., *Scriptural Truth About The Lord's Return*. Westwood, New Jersey: Fleming H. Revell, 1922.

Chafer, Lewis Sperry, *Satan And The Satanic System*. Chicago: Moody Press, 1945.

__________, *The Kingdom In History And Prophecy*. Grand Rapids: Zondervan Publishing Co., n.d.

__________, *Major Bible Themes*. Dallas: Dallas Theological Seminary, 1953.

Cooper, D. L., *Messiah, His Nature And Person*. Los Angeles: Biblical Research Society, 1933.

__________, *The God Of Israel*. Los Angeles: Biblical Research Society, 1945.

Culbertson, W. And Centz, H. B., *Understanding The Times*. Grand Rapids: Zondervan Publishing Co., 1956.

DeHaan, Martin R., *The Second Coming Of Jesus*. Grand Rapids: Zondervan Publishing Co., 1944.

Dodd, C. H., *The Coming Of Christ*. New York: Cambridge University Press, 1958.

__________, *The Parables Of The Kingdom*. New York: Scribners, 1961.

English, E. Schuyler, *Rethinking The Rapture*. Travelers Rest, South Carolina: Southern Bible Book House, c. 1954.

Erb, P., *The Alpha And The Omega.* Scottdale, Pennsylvania: Herald Press, 1955.

Erdman, Charles R., *The Return Of Christ.* New York: George H. Doran, 1922.

Erdman, W. J., *Notes On The Revelation* (ed., C. R. Erdman). New York: Fleming H. Revell, 1930.

Feinberg, C. L., Premillennialism Or Amillennialism. Grand Rapids: Zondervan Publishing Co., 1936.

Fowler, C. L., *Building The Dispensations.* Denver: Maranatha Press, 1940.

Froom, Leslie E., *The Prophetic Faith Of Our Fathers.* Washington, D.C.: Review And Herald Publishing Co., 1950.

Frost, H. W., *Matthew Twenty-Four And The Revelation.* New York: Oxford University Press, 1924.

Gaebelein, Arno C., *Harmony Of The Prophetic Word.* New York: Fleming H. Revell, 1907.

————————————, *Hath God Cast Away His People?* New York: Gospel Publishing House, n.d.

————————————, *The Return Of The Lord.* New York: Our Hope Publishers, n.d.

Girdlestone, R. B., *The Grammar Of Prophecy.* Grand Rapids: Kregel Publications, 1955.

Glasson, T. F., *His Appearing And His Kingdom.* London: Epworth Press, 1953.

Grant, F. W., *Man And The Future State.* New York: Loizeaux Brothers, n.d.

Grier, W. J., *The Momentous Event.* Belfast: Evangelical Bookshop, 1945.

Guinness, H. Grattan, *Light For the Last Days.* London: Marshall, Morgan & Scott, 1917.

————————————, *The Approaching End Of The Age.* London: Hodder & Stoughton, 1882.

Haldeman, I. M., *The Coming Of Christ.* Grand Rapids: Baker Book House, 1963 (Reprint).

Hamilton, F. E., *The Basis Of Millennial Faith.* Grand
    Rapids: Wm. B. Eerdmans Publishing Co., 1952.
Hislop, A. *The Two Babylons.* Neptune, New Jersey:
    Loizeaux Bros., 1943.
Hodges, J. W., *Christ's Kingdom And Coming.* Grand
    Rapids: Wm. B. Eerdmans Publishing Co., 1957.
Hogg, C. F. And Vine, W. E., *Touching The Coming Of
    The Lord.* Edinburgh And London: Oliphants, 1919.
Houghton, T., *The Faith And Hope Of The Future.* No
    city: The Evangelical Fellowship, n.d.
Hughes, A., *A New Heaven And A New Earth.* Philadel-
    phia: Presbyterian And Reformed Publishing Co., 1958.

Ironside, Harry A., *The Great Parenthesis.* Grand Rapids:
    Zondervan Publishing Co., 1943.
——————————————, *The Lamp Of Prophecy.* Grand Rapids:
    Zondervan Publishing Co., 1962.

Jennings, F. C., *Satan, His Person, Work, Place and Destiny.*
    New York: Our Hope Publishers, n.d.

Kellogg, S. H., *Are Premillennialists Right?* New York:
    Fleming H. Revell, 1923.
Kelly, William, *Lectures On The Second Coming And King-
    dom Of Our Lord And Saviour Jesus Christ.* New York:
    Loizeaux Brothers, n.d.
Kraus, C. N. *Dispensationalism In America.* Richmond,
    Virginia: John Knox Press, 1958.
Kromminga, D. H., *Millennium In The Church.* Grand
    Rapids: Wm. B. Eerdmans Publishing Co., 1945.

Ladd, George Eldon, *Crucial Questions About The Kingdom
    Of God.* Grand Rapids: Wm. B. Eerdmans., 1952.

——————————————, *The Blessed Hope.* Grand Rapids: Wm.
    B. Eerdmans Publishing Co., 1956.
——————————————, *The Gospel Of The Kingdom.* Grand
    Rapids: Wm. B. Eerdmans Publishing Co., 1959.

Langston, E. L., *Ominous Days*. London: Chas. J. Thynne & Jarvis, 1925.

Larkin, Clarence, *Dispensational Truth*. Philadelphia: Clarence Larkin Estate, c. 1918.

Mackintosh, C. H., *Papers On The Lord's Coming*. New York: Loizeaux Brothers, 1898.

McClain, Alvah J., *The Greatness Of The Kingdom*. Grand Rapids: Zondervan Publishing Co., 1959.

Masselink, William, *Why Thousand Years?* Grand Rapids: Wm. B. Eerdmans Publishing Co., 1930.

Mauro, Phillip, *Looking For the Saviour*. London: Samuel E. Roberts, 1913.

——————————————, *The Gospel Of The Kingdom*. No city: Hamilton Brothers, 1928.

——————————————, *The Patmos Vision*. Boston: The Scripture Truth Depot, c. 1925.

——————————————, *The Kingdom Of Heaven*. Swengel, Pennsylvania: Reiner Publications, n.d.

Middleton, R., *How Is Jesus Coming?* London: Marshall Brothers Ltd., 1898.

Minear, P. S., *Christian Hope And The Second Coming*. Philadelphia: Westminster, 1954.

Moore, R. W. B., *The Nearness Of The Lord's Return*. London: Robert Scott, 1913.

Morgan, G. Campbell, *God's Methods With Man*. New York: Fleming H. Revell, 1898.

Muller, J. J., *When Christ Comes Again*. London: Marshall, Morgan & Scott, 1956.

Munhall, L. W., *The Lord's Return*. Grand Rapids: Kregel Publications, 1962.

Newton, B. W., *Thoughts On The Apocalypse*. London: Houlston & Sons, 1904.

Norris, H., *The End Of The Age, How And When?* Bath, England: Advent Herald Publishing House, n.d.

Ottman, Ford C., *The Unfolding Of The Ages.*   Grand Rapids: Kregel Publications, 1967.

Otto, Rudolf, *The Kingdom of God And The Son Of Man.* London: Lutterworth Press, 1943.

Pache, René, *The Return Of Jesus Christ.* Chicago: Moody Press, 1955.

Panton, D. M., *Rapture.* London: Chas. J. Thynne, 1922.

Payne, J. Barton, *The Imminent Appearing Of Christ.* Grand Rapids: Wm. B. Eerdmans Publishing Co., 1962.

Pember, G. A., *Earth's Earliest Ages.* New York: Fleming H. Revell, n.d.

————————————, *The Great Prophecies.* New York: Christian Herald Office, 1887.

Pentecost, J. Dwight, *Things To Come.* Findlay, Ohio: Dunham Publishing Co., 1958.

Peters, G. N. H., *The Theocratic Kingdom Of Our Lord Jesus Christ.* Grand Rapids: Kregel Publications, 1952.

Reese, A., *The Approaching Advent Of Christ.* London: Marshall, Morgan & Scott, n.d.

Ridderbos, Herman, *The Coming Of The Kingdom.* Philadelphia: Presbyterian And Reformed Publishing Co., 1962.

Robertson, F. W., "*The Transitoriness of Life,*" from *Sermons Preached at Brighton.* New York: Harper & Bros., n.d.

Robinson, John A. T., *Jesus And His Coming.* Nashville Abingdon, 1958.

Robinson, W. C., *Christ, The Hope Of Glory.* Grand Rapids: Wm. B. Eerdmans Publishing Co., 1945

Rowley, H. H., *The Relevance of the Apocalyptic.* London: Lutterworth Press, 1963.

Ryrie, Charles, *Dispensationalism Today.* Chicago: Moody Press, 1965.

————————————, *The Basis Of The Premillennial Faith* New York: Loizeaux Brothers, 1953.

Schaff, Philip, *History of the Christian Church*. New York: Chas. Scribner's Sons, 1907.

Schweitzer, A., *The Mystery of the Kingdom of God*. London; A & C Black, Ltd., 1963.

Scofield, Cyrus I., *Rightly Dividing The Word Of Truth*. New York: Fleming H. Revell, 1896.

——————————, *Prophecy Made Plain*. Glasgow: Pickering & Inglis, n.d.

Scott W., *At Hand*. Glasgow: Pickering & Inglis, n.d.

——————————, *Exposition Of The Revelation Of Jesus Christ*. Glasgow: Pickering & Inglis, n.d.

——————————, *Prophetic Scenes And Coming Glories*. New York: Loizeaux Brothers, n.d.

Silver, J. F., *The Lord's Return*. New York: Fleming H. Revell, 1941.

Smith, W. M., *Egypt In Biblical History*. Boston: W. A. Wilde & Co., 1957.

Soltau, George, *The Plan Of The Ages*. London: John A. Roberts Publishing Co., n.d.

Stanton, G. B., *Kept From The Hour*. Grand Rapids: Zondervan Publishing Co., 1956.

Strombeck, J. F., *First The Rapture*. Moline, Illinois: Strombeck Agency, 1950.

Tatford, Fredrick A., *Prophecy's Last Word*. London: Pickering & Inglis, 1947.

——————————, *The Climax Of The Ages*. London: Oliphants, Ltd., 1953.

——————————, *The Faith*. London: Pickering & Inglis, 1952.

——————————, *The Person And Work Of The Devil*. London: Hulbert Publishing Co., n.d.

——————————, *The Prince of Darkness*. Eastbourne, England, B.A.T.M., 1967.

Thiessen, H. C., *Will the Church Pass Through the Tribulation?* New York: Loizeaux Bros., 1941.

Torrey, Reuben A., *The Return Of The Lord Jesus*. Grand Rapids: Baker Book House, 1966.

Tregelles, S. P., *The Hope Of Christ's Second Coming.* London: Sovereign Grace Advent Testimony, 1964.

Trench, G. F., *After The Thousand Years.* London: Morgan And Scott, 1844.

Trotter, W., *Plain Papers On Prophetic Subjects.* New York: Loizeaux Brothers, n.d.

Unger, M. F., *Great Neglected Bible Prophecies.* Wheaton, Illinois: Scripture Press, 1955.

Vine, W. E., *An Expository Dictionary of New Testament Words.* London, Oliphants, n.d.

Vos, G., *Pauline Eschatology.* Grand Rapids: Wm. B. Eerdmans Publishing Co., 1952.

————————————, *The Kingdom And The Church.* Grand Rapids: Wm. B. Eerdmans Publishing Co., n.d.

Walvoord, J. F., *The Millennial Kingdom.* Grand Rapids: Dunham Publishing Co., 1959.

————————————, *The Return Of The Lord.* Grand Rapids: Dunham Publishing Co., 1964.

Ware, A. E., *The Hour Of Translation.* London & Edinburgh: Marshall & Co., 1932.

West, Nathaniel, *Daniel's Great Prophecy.* New York: Fleming H. Revell, 1898.

————————————, *The Thousand Years In Both Testaments.* Fincastle, Virginia: Scripture Truth Book Co., 1966.

Wilkinson, S. H., *The Israel Promises And Their Fulfillment.* London: 1936.

Wood, Leon J., *Is The Rapture Next?* Grand Rapids: Zondervan Publishing Co., 1956.

Wuest, Kenneth S., *Prophetic Light In the Present Darkness.* Grand Rapids: Wm. B. Eerdmans Publishing Co., 1955.

Zorn, R. O., *Church And Kingdom.* Philadelphia: Presbyterian And Reformed Publishing Co., 1962.